# COWBELLS AND COFFINS

## THE OLD GENERAL STORE

### Mary Frances Beverley

Foreword by Tumbleweed Smith

EAKIN PRESS · Fort Worth, Texas
www.EakinPress.com

*To Kimberly*

Library of Congress Cataloging-in-Publication Data

Beverley, Mary Frances.
    Cowbells and coffins.

    Bibliography: p.
    Includes index.
    1. General stores — United States — History.  I. Title.
HF5429.3.B49   1987   381'.1   87-6711
ISBN 0-89015-593-3 (pbk.)

# Contents

# Foreword

While most owners of general stores refer to post offices being in their stores, Hondo Crouch always said his combination store and beer joint was in the post office. "But we have a white line on the floor,' Hondo explained, "and you can't drink beer past the white line. 'Cause that's in the post office and we kinda respect the flag and all that. So that's why we don't drink beer in the post office." When asked what items he sold in his store, Hondo replied simply, "Post Toasties and singletrees and Argo starch, pots, pans, buckets, slop jars and powder."

Hondo enjoyed his customers: "Little lady came in the other day and wanted some fresh peaches. I showed her where they were. She said, 'My goodness, they're awfully small.' I told her that was all we had, so she took 'em. Bright and early the next morning she was back and told me: 'Not only were they small, they were absolutely tasteless.' I said to her, 'Well, it's a good thing they were small.' "

Hondo's antics were legendary, but his character was not too different from owners of general stores. Most have a fine sense of humor. They have to because running a store means hard work, long hours, and little pay. All sorts of problems crop up, but through them all, store owners possess an amazingly profound respect and reverence for life. They feel quite at home in their stores and, like royalty, delight in ruling over their domains. Usually just being in the presence of the store owner made the early pioneers feel better. The owner gave his customers assurance that all was well with the world, that the ground was still beneath their feet, April would come again, and they all had lots to be thankful for. Sometimes the store owner was not paid for goods some customers bought on credit because of hard times, but somehow that brought the store owner even more respect.

The old plank flooring in their stores, although swaying with the memories, has withstood the wear and tear of decades. The old set of scales has weighed tons of merchandise. Plenty of children and adults alike took their first elevator rides in a rope and pulley-powered freight elevator going from the main floor to the basement in an old country store.

Early store owners were benefactors to fledgling schools, churches, and lodges. Some stores carried bold slogans such as "The Store That Carries Everything" and came close to doing just that. The stores served trade areas covering hundreds of miles and at times, freight haulers would drive their wagons and teams great distances to get to the store. If they arrived at night, they thought nothing of napping on the porch of the store. Sometimes, in anticipation of the freighter's arrival, the store may have been unlocked. The freighters might return home with five wagons full of merchandise, enough to last a year.

Candy was a scarce commodity in most early stores. About the only kind was a peanut patty. These were displayed, unwrapped, in a wooden box with a moist towel over it to preserve freshness. Youngsters loved to explore the upstairs of stores. No telling what they might find. But it was always a scary adventure. For the older men in the community, the store was a great meeting place because the owner, as host, provided a welcome atmosphere and free snacks of pickles, cheese, and other delicacies. Store owners knew all their customers and their kids, their horses, dogs, and wagons.

The stores had a particular look, smell, and feel. The shelves and counters are now dark with experience and age, carrying imprints where millions of community elbows have rested. The old stores, with their weathered boards and weathered people, give us a glimpse of forgotten times. And if you listen real hard you can hear some echoes of an era of brass bands, the boy rolling a hoop with a stick, the family eating fresh homemade ice cream on the front porch while the cat naps in the swing, a trellis of honey-suckle providing shade. Hear the quiet excitement of a time when people shouted hooray and were proud to be alive in America.

What more could you expect from places with names like A. Sherley & Bros, Bergheim General Store and Post Office, or the Audra Mercantile? Mary Frances Beverley went to these and many more stores, crossing the country, meeting people, soaking up the local color. It is easy to find a certain fascination in visiting a few general stores, but Mary Frances, who has been in more of the old stores than most people, approached each one like it was the first one she had ever seen. She brought the same childlike enchantment to her typewriter as she prepared this unique book. It's my pleasure to recommend it and be a part of it.

TUMBLEWEED SMITH

# Preface

Whether it faces the empty railroad tracks in the center of town or fronts the highway with gasoline pumps added years after it was built, or whether it sits on Main Street opposite the courthouse square, in hundreds of small American towns, the place that has survived the longest as the fingerprint of the community is the general merchandise store.

Many of these stores have closed or are holding on by only a cobweb, victims of a variety of changes that have taken away their customers. Yet a surprising number exist where storekeepers open their doors before sunrise every morning, stay open past dark, and carry "everything from the cradle to the grave," just as their fathers, grandfathers, and even their great-grandfathers did.

From the mid-1800s through the first quarter of this century, the general store was the hearthstone of the community, the backdrop for a way of life common to small towns everywhere. Even today, people regularly visit the surviving stores, not merely to shop but to exchange pieces of their lives, to learn who has a new baby, who is ill, who is getting married, who died. On the nicked-up benches outside, men may not whittle as much as they used to, but they still talk about the same things their grandfathers discussed: the weather, prices of crops and land, mistakes of government and public officials. In wintertime they still sit inside, play a game of dominoes, and lean toward a wood-burning stove for warmth. Maybe in some places they even still argue about religion.

Many of the first stores were preceded by trading posts in settlements where both Indians and whites bartered goods. The first business established in a new community was usually a general store. Many towns took the names of stores as their own — Guys Store, Truetts Store, today only highway signs marking the sites that are now only a few scattered houses.

Next to fires, the most prophetic influence on any town's future was the location of the railroad, followed by the location of the county seat, the highway, and, in more recent years, the highway loop. When a highway was rerouted, perhaps moved only a few hundred yards from its original location, some stores were forced to reverse their entrances so that their front doors, which formerly faced the road, became their back doors. That was not such a drastic alteration, but stores that once faced the main road could find themselves empty as people took the new highway or interstate to a larger town to shop. At the same time, highways built in recent years alongside old stores have brought new life in tourist trade from the road.

The first post offices were often located within the general stores. Frequently, the store owner was also a town's postmaster. Some former stores that no longer have enough business to operate with a complete stock remain open today only because they serve as the community's post office. In these silent little buildings, the postmaster often uses the original brass postal boxes and serves customers through the same brass grille windows.

Many of the early mercantile stores served as their towns' first banks, often in a corner of the store inside handsome wood enclosures with ornate tellers' windows. Banker-merchants exchanged credit for prospective crops, sometimes issuing metal tokens with cash value. At the end of the month, accounts would be settled that had been registered in a thick ledger or on little white pads, stored upright in a wooden box or in a black metal McCaskey file. Today, while the name in gold block letters across the top may not be the same as that of the current store owner, old black safes with hand-painted pastoral scenes on their doors still protect the store's valuables.

Many early-century stores sold coffins and offered funeral home services to the townspeople, sometimes employing a mortician. An embalming room was often upstairs and an ornately carved hearse kept out back. Old store ledgers that list "casket handles" but not caskets suggest that the town's coffins were made by a local carpenter. Some store museums and stores still in business have saved their old wooden coffins, coffin stands, and women's yellowed silk burial gowns, still in their boxes.

The general store was a town's first news center. Besides news exchanged between customers, the first, and — for a while — the only telephone in town was in the store. Longtime store owners recall how commonplace it was to deliver messages, no matter how far out in the country they had to go. Now, as in years past, families tack black-bordered funeral notices outside the store's front door, announcing the exact time of death, age of the deceased (including years, months, and days), time and place for the funeral, and where friends might view the body. Today's store bulletin boards alongside weather-beaten front doors may include notes to describe a lost dog ("Old Blue's real gentle"), tell townfolk where they can buy a good horse or post hole diggers ("worth the price"), or announce a church supper ("Everybody come!"). The store may also be the central contact for reporting fires to the town's volunteer fire department.

Whether at a Tennessee crossroads, on a town square in Iowa, in an Oklahoma hamlet, or facing a major roadway in Texas, virtually every general store in the country built between the mid-1800s and the beginning of this century was almost identical. In design, contents, and in the storekeeper's method of operation and his attitude toward his customers, through them all runs a common thread.

The first stores in established towns usually had either the false-front "Alamo" shape or were two-story, barn-shaped structures. Owners who stayed in business over a period of years were often forced to rebuild at least once because of fires. When a merchant rebuilt, he used brick or stone, and often added cast-iron doorplates or marble cornerstones that preserved his name and the year his new store opened.

Interiors of the early stores usually featured either beaded ceilings of narrow wood strips or fanciful pressed tin, painted silver or white. Solid oak floors were designed to last more than a lifetime — and many have. Standard furnishings found in countless old stores today, now antiques and "NOT FOR SALE" (you needn't ask), include a heavy National or Michigan cash register; ceiling-high track ladders running the store's length; a wheel cheesecutter; brass or white porcelain scales; long, glass-enclosed display counters; glass-fronted bins for peas, rice, and beans; a coffee grinder; a tobacco cutter; a kerosene pump that filled "coal oil" lamps and was also used for medicinal purposes; and perhaps inside every store ever built, a revolving, octagonal-shaped, oak hardware cabinet.

On the faded, rusty signs, both outside and inside these old stores, you can read the history of what America has used and enjoyed — at least, that is, the things that were most often advertised. Bread companies and funeral homes donated benches with their names on them to put on the porch or inside by the stove. Screen doors and store walls beckoned customers to buy Nehi, Grapette, a Winchester rifle, Dr. LeGear's Cow and Horse Prescription, Black Draught, and Star Tobacco.

The store's wide selection of merchandise foretold our modern-day supermarkets. Larger stores had two sections, one holding groceries, hardware, tobacco, medicines, feed, and seed, and another side containing such items as bolts of fabric, thread, overalls, shirts, shoes, hats, and gloves.

An 1883 store ledger listed among its sales to one customer a revealing description of the lifestyle of that community and thousands like it: calico, gingham, velvet, outing flannel, braid, gloves, drawers, shirts, snuff, matches, goblets, soap, lye, lard, bacon, coal, eggs, vinegar, "sirup," apples, flour, coffee mill, seed, shovels, and brooms. Heavy, ragged ledgers and other records are often moving diaries of events that affected an entire town or region. Ledgers that survived fires, floods, storms, and economic depressions reflect in blank pages and skipped dates the effects of a disaster on a store.

Storekeepers have always been good businessmen, willing listeners, reliable local historians, community leaders, and above-average givers of directions. Most still work long hours and pride themselves on the personal attention they give each customer:

"It's the way my granddaddy did it."

They still carry many of the items that their fathers and grandfathers carried: cowbells, rope, feed, local produce, hardware, washboards, brooms, horse collars, overalls, straw hats, kerosene lamps, chamber pots, and woodstoves. There is still a demand for these things, especially in the rural areas of the country. Some third-generation owners want to show you treasured photographs of the store in the early days when the road out front was dirt, yellowed grocery ads when salmon was seventeen cents a can, or their big, square icebox with its mirrored doors, electric now but in the old days cooled with block ice. Many small-town merchants still observe the old customs, closing for a townsman's funeral, carrying customers' charge accounts, even lending money on occasion.

A small town's general store is still the hub of activity for homecomings, fairs, and reunions. Some have earned distinctions of their own, such as the Texas crossroads store that became immortalized when Willie Nelson and Waylon Jennings recorded "Let's Go Back to Luckenbach, Texas."

The "movie people," as the small-town residents call them, have discovered real, open-for-business general stores for film locations. Locals work willingly as extras, and with all those old wagons and other antiques around, the film makers hardly ever have to bring in any props. They just rent what is already there. As one elderly storekeeper said, a little smugly, "The Disney people wanted to buy everything I've got, but I wouldn't sell. Just rented 'em out."

Throughout the country, former general mercantile stores that are no longer in business as stores now house shops, museums, restaurants, and other businesses. In Fredericksburg, Texas, Main Street is a history of early merchandising in the lovingly preserved limestone buildings built by the early German settlers. Other former stores are being used as general store museums, filled with some of the original merchandise and other authentic contents.

For every store still open and prospering in places with names that echo their origins — Bergheim, Boone, Cherokee, Lajitas — dozens, possibly hundreds, are sitting, held tenuously together by splinters and shadows and somebody's memories. The owner may sit alone every day, staring at the empty aisles, keeping the door open perhaps as a defiant gesture against the new highway or the chain stores or whatever thief stole his customers away — or maybe only to preserve a place for him to go each morning. Fragments of things that people once needed or wanted lie shrouded in dust in random clutter on glass display cases and high shelves. Almost-new merchandise was put out so long ago, it too wears a whispery gray layer of time.

Probably no one puts up much of a fuss when one of these old stores is torn down and replaced with a new highway, telephone company building, or parking lot. But before they are all gone, taking with them all the things we used and enjoyed and valued in this little wink on history's calendar, you might want to go take a look. And bring your children.

You'd better hurry.

# Acknowledgments

For their generous assistance, I want to express my sincerest appreciation to the following: Bob Lewis (Tumbleweed Smith), Jim Beverly, Walter Pate AIA, Myra McIlvain, Elise Kowert, Evelyn Faist, Donna Bennett, Moody Anderson, Tom Copeland, and all the county extension agents who led me to old stores. Thanks also to staff members of the Eugene C. Barker Texas History Center, University of Texas at Austin; the Fredericksburg Public Library Texana Collection; Jacksonville Public Library; Midland County Library; Nita Stewart Haley Library, Midland; Lajitas Research Library; the Comfort Library; Bertram Chamber of Commerce; and all the general store owners and their families mentioned in this book for sharing with me their memories.

# 1 Bergheim General Store and Post Office

*Andreas Engel rebuilt his original store in 1903, using stone hauled to the location in mule-drawn wagons. He named his little settlement Bergheim, which means "home in the hills."*

*Trading cedar posts for groceries — my biggest mistake.*

— Andreas Engel

BERGHEIM Store owner and postmaster Stanley Jones can appreciate the steady business his store enjoys today. He owns his great-grandfather Andreas Engel's record of Bergheim's early days when times were not easy. Engel, an Austrian immigrant, established his first store in 1892, and his story of floods, freezing winters, and Depression days paints a realistic picture of what it must have been like to be a merchant back then.

Engel named the little settlement Bergheim, which means "home in the hills." It is located about thirty miles north of San Antonio at the intersection of the roads to Boerne, Blanco, and New Braunfels. The site is as beautiful as the name suggests, but in those days, Andreas and his wife Eva probably had very little time to enjoy the scenery.

Over and over, in the history of the store that Engel wrote, he describes details of the weather and its effects on his business. The winter of 1887 was one of the coldest the entire state had ever known. Cattle froze, and everyone suffered. The first year of the twentieth century was a wet one, with a July flood which caused further devastation. In 1903 Engel rebuilt the store on higher ground, using stone hauled to the location in mule-drawn wagons

*General mercantile stores were the first supermarkets, selling groceries, clothing, canning jars, hardware, cowbells, and even coffins.*

by rock mason William Stendebach.

Soon Engel's son Alfred was part of the business. Old cotton ginners' record books speak for themselves of good and not-so-good years which followed.

Charge accounts for customers from the surrounding area were kept then in the McCaskey System accounts receivable box. The dusty old box sits today near the 1903 cash register from the National Cash Register Company of Dayton, Ohio. Great-grandson Jones still uses the cash register but keeps his charge accounts on ordinary receipt pads in a large cardboard box.

In a cabinet at the back of the store, old medicines that were sold in the past are on display but are not for sale. Included are treatments and cures for people and animals alike: Dr. LeGear's Stock

Powders "for dairy cows, horses, cattle, sheep, and hogs"; Dogie Brand Wormide for screwworms; Black Draught Laxative; Shiloh Cough Syrup; Dr. Fenner's Golden Relief for colic, "to be used externally for minor cuts and bruises, and sore muscles"; Dr. Thatcher's Uterina, "antiseptic wash tablets to be used while taking Stella Vitae as directed on page 10 of *Our Wives and Daughters Book.*" According to the outside of the box, Dr. Thatcher's was also good for sore throats and for use as a nasal spray. In an old glass case you can see other items which sold well: razors and razor blades, Blackstone Aspirin, Fitch's Talc, Crystal White Family Soap, Old Dutch Cleanser, Octagon Laundry Soap, and Texas Girl Drip Coffee.

In 1912 gasoline was in great demand, and at first it was sold from large drums with spigots. Customers brought their own containers to carry the gas home. Probably one of the biggest decisions storekeepers had to make was when it was time to remove the hitching posts for good and install gasoline pumps.

Cotton ginning in the area ended in 1928, and Engel devotes many pages to the hard days of the Depression. He tells how he started trading cedar posts for groceries because no one could sell the cedar. He calls it "my biggest mistake."

As you walk around the crowded old store, you are surrounded by a paradoxical jumble of the old and the new. Look up at the top shelves near the original beaded ceiling and see some old scales next to a wooden Hires Root Beer case. A bit lower your glance takes in tins of Red Man and Skoal chewing tobacco, modern sunglasses, head scarves, and a Lone Star beer sign. A local farmer stands by the boxes of fresh onions, potatoes, and watermelons on the old oak floor, waiting to pay for two loaves of Mrs. Baird's bread. Behind you, in thick stacks across the top of the old nail bins, still filled with nails for sale, are blue jeans, straw cowboy hats and, at the end of the counter, canning jars. You can even borrow a book from the store's lending library, and T-shirts for sale let you tell everyone "I shopped the Mall in Bergheim, Texas."

The Bergheim Store is open from 7:30 A.M. until 7:00 P.M. The busiest time may be around 6:00 P.M., when even more customers stop by for a six-pack, flashlight batteries, milk, maybe some fence wire. Some things don't change: they also pick up freshly laid brown eggs, sausage on a stick, homemade tamales, and fried pies.

It is doubtful that Stanley Jones will ever have to take cedar posts in exchange for groceries as his grandfather and great-grandfather did, and it looks as if the old charge account system still works just fine.

# 2 | A. B. McGill & Company

*Mr. McGill would advance them what they needed, then when their crop came in . . . we'd even up.*
— Ben Warden

BERTRAM   Towns the railroad bypassed did not always accept with grace being jilted. Some of them simply packed their bags and followed the railroad to a new location right alongside its tracks. This is how the town of Bertram came to be — and to be where it is.

During the early 1870s in Central Texas, the little settlement of South Gabriel was building "A Town of Worth" with stores, a rock schoolhouse, hotel, wagon shop, cotton gin, and saloon. By 1880, T. S. Reed had assumed management of Melvin Lockett's mercantile store there. Then, the Austin and Northwestern Railroad began laying their tracks, heading northward from Austin toward Burnet. Their plans were to miss South Gabriel by two miles. The railroad company was quickly offered $3,000 to change their plans and come through South Gabriel, but the offer was emphatically refused.

Not to be spurned, the citizens of South Gabriel moved thirteen of their homes and two stores to the present site of Bertram. It took thirteen yoke of oxen and numerous wagons two days to move the town to land owned by T. D. Vaughan. T. S. Reed dismantled the South Gabriel schoolhouse and moved the stones to Bertram for his mercantile store facing the railroad tracks. They named the town Bertram after Rudolph Bertram, a prominent Austin merchant.

By 1882, Bertram had a post office and other stores and businesses. During its first decade, hundreds of railroad cars hauling pink granite from near Marble Falls rumbled past the store, destined for the state capitol at Austin.

Malcolm and Dave Reed became a part of the store operation with their father in 1898, and shortly afterwards, the elder Reed moved to Beaumont to run a wholesale-retail grocery business. Later, Malcolm moved to Marble Falls and became a

*Like dozens of general stores all over the country, no one wants to run Nettie Whipple's store any more. Nettie herself was almost ninety-three when she stopped cutting piece goods and selling jars of honey from the hives in her own back yard.*

well-known merchant there.

In 1905 Dave Reed was the sole owner of the little rock Bertram store and that year erected a two-story, sandstone and broken-face limestone structure next door. Its builder, Ray McDonald, marked the date with a black marble cornerstone.

Since many of the first mercantile stores also acted as banks, issuing credit tokens to be exchanged for merchandise, the next most natural step

*Ben Warden was only nineteen when he began working in the McGill store as a bank teller.*

was for them to incorporate actual banking services such as the advancing of cash to customers, to be used for goods bought in the store.

As the store's banking business grew, Dave Reed brought in as a partner his brother-in-law, Brown McGill. Reed then moved to Austin, leaving McGill the store's owner. In 1939 the store was taken over by Ada Reed Brewer and her husband Bob Brewer, who still operate it.

During the early part of the century, children going to the general store with their mothers to buy new school clothes looked forward to a new pair of Buster Brown shoes. In real life, Buster Brown was Bertram's Johnny Clifton, a midget who, with his dog Tige, traveled all over the United States promoting Buster Brown Shoes. Around 1908, Johnny returned to his hometown and made an appearance with Tige on a platform in front of the McGill store. A crowd gathered, the men wearing wide, western-style hats, the women in large sunbonnets with the ties hanging down their backs. Other spectators hung out the store's second-floor windows to see the famous pair.

The year 1914 was a milestone for Bertram. Cotton had been the primary crop in the area for some time, but that year, farmers around the town brought in 10,000 bales to be ginned. No doubt McGill's store also profited from the crop. An interior photograph of the store made that year shows the wide, graceful staircase with double newel posts, leading up to the second floor where Alma Ross had her millinery shop. Also on the second floor, Thurlow Weed, the Austin undertaker, made funeral arrangements for Bertram families who bought coffins from the store. In the photo, standing in the spacious store, well-stocked with canned goods, brooms, hardware, and clothing, are A. B. Marcus, Emzy Marcus, and Brown McGill, each wearing a long-sleeved white shirt and a bow tie.

Stroll around the store today, and it isn't hard to picture the three men there again, even if the store is more crowded and stocked with different kinds of merchandise, the wide stairs now cluttered with boxes. A sweeping look reveals the closest thing to an old-fashioned department store you are apt to find nowadays. No plows nor feed nor eggs in wooden crates, but attractive clothing, shoes, men's hats, fine giftware, and electrical appliances can be found. Here and there your eye is stopped by an item that seems to have been delivered to the store by mistake in some sort of time warp or left over from a sale a half century ago — or more: a child's convertible rocker/high chair; an Edison Morning Glory gramaphone; an iron beehive string holder; and two pairs of the narrowest, most pointed-toed (did women actually *wear* these?) shoes, laced up the ankle.

The old furnishings somehow blend in with the

store's modern contents: the big, wood and glass Merrick's Spool Cotton thread case; a large, glass-sided case with double racks for ribbon; a counter with glass-fronted bins that once held rice, beans, and peas; and in the shoe department, two seats for trying on shoes, on their backs "Star Brand Shoes Are Better." The big elevator at the back of the store once carried to the second floor big sacks of flour, coffins, and other bulky merchandise for storage. The heavy cash registers in the store will probably last forever.

Tucked away in a back corner is the store office, once the enclosure for the bank within the store. The handsome wood and brass work, crafted by the Nalle Company of Austin, is still beautiful. Heavy brass grillwork extended the wood to a higher level, and the Brewers removed the grillwork but are thinking of replacing it. One opening served as a place for customers to pay for their purchases, another as the bank teller's window. Inside, a classic black-and-gold safe door from the Mosler Safe Company features a peaceful, handpainted lake scene. Bold letters above the door state that the owner is "D. C. Reed & Co."

Near the office enclosure rests a ninety-six-drawer, octagonal, oak hardware cabinet, its porcelain knobs still sparkling. Next to it, tall white scales from the drug store around the corner ask "What Is Your Wate Today?"

Seeking out the history and essence of a place often depends upon fragmentary memories and stories that have been repeated so often, they have lost their original accuracy. Not in Bertram. If you need to know what the early days of the store and the town were like, you talk to Benjamin Franklin Warden. In 1986 Ben was ninety years old, and not many people can remember yesterday as well as Ben remembers the store's brightest, busiest days more than half a century ago.

Ben had just graduated from Bertram's big, new, red-brick school — as valedictorian. He was twenty years old when one day McGill called Ben's father. It was 1915. Ben smiles a lot when he talks, whether at himself or at the events he is relating, a listener can't tell, but he remembers that when he came to the telephone to see what Mr. McGill wanted, Ben said, "Howdy." He thought McGill wanted him to come work as a cashier. Actually, he wanted Ben to be the bank teller.

Ben can tell you which door he entered when he came to work every morning (one of the big front doors) and how most of the customers used the back door or the side door by the bank section because there was no road out front at first. He also remembers the time the schoolchildren got "the itch." They were paying for purchases with hands that were broken out, so Ben and his co-workers behind the cashier's and teller's windows washed their hands in formaldehyde several times a day so they wouldn't catch it. They didn't.

He has no trouble remembering when people were good about paying their bills, and when they put up cotton and cattle as collateral. "Mr. McGill would advance them what they needed, then when their crop came in, I'd figure it all out, and we'd even up."

Under the drawer pulls behind the teller's window where Ben worked, the dark stain on the wood has been rubbed away. The floor behind the bank windows is covered now with carpet to protect the hardwood floors worn down by years of Reeds and McGills and Brewers tending to store business.

A white-haired Bertram gentleman comes into the store, looking for a new shirt. He is introduced to me as Dr. Connell. He tells me he has been shopping at McGill's for many years, and yes, he too remembers Buster Brown.

Before I leave Bertram, with its curious but appealing blend of ghost town and thriving little town, I ask a few people: "What are you proudest of here? What would you want people to know about your town?" No one could think of a single thing. I am astonished — and disappointed.

They could have named Ben Warden or the Brewers or the McGills or the Reeds — or especially those resolute South Gabriel folk who would not let the railroad pass them by.

# 3 | Audra Mercantile Store

*Here's something else you won't know. It's a wash boiler. . . . I've seen Mama use that a hundred times!*
— Opal Hunt

BRADSHAW   The Audra Mercantile Store still carries a few groceries and modern-day items, but it isn't a store you would ever want to step into without a clear shopping list. Its high-ceilinged rooms are filled with distractions, reminders of a way of life years gone by.

Remembering those years is what Opal Hunt does best. The eighty-four-year-old storekeeper has been around the Audra Mercantile since 1909, when her father moved a small frame building to this location in the little community of Bradshaw, south of Abilene. He named the store after the settlement to the west where Opal was born. In 1912 he replaced the small store with the present brick building, and today it is Bradshaw's only remaining business.

Opal loves to talk about the store, the town, and her memories. She can tell you about the red-brick bank across the side street where her brother worked. She remembers when the collapsing variety store across the street was run by the Dankworth brothers, who called it a "racket store." There was a time, she recalls, when the big square church on the corner was filled with people every Sunday.

Originally a stop on the Abilene and Southern Railroad, Bradshaw was never very big, maybe 300 residents at its peak, with a barber shop, a meat market, a drug store, two doctors, and two cotton gins. Cotton was the reason for Bradshaw's existence. Today, Opal's customers are the few remaining townspeople, along with frequent travelers who hear about the store from others who discover it, often accidentally. Opal's guest book lists visitors from all over the world.

The small, lively woman speaks with affection of her parents, Julia and Meno Hunt, and leads me around the huge, old store to point out mementos from her family, things they owned and used and some of the things they sold. On a shelf are faded boxes of Dr. LeGear's Stock Powder and Cow Prescription; on a wall, time-dusted harness and rope, nearby a flour barrel with "Audra Mercantile" still faintly visible. As Opal points out the old candy scales — "where Papa used to weigh me!" — and the wooden platform where big sacks of grain were stacked — "where I played when I was little!" — I

*Opal Hunt grew up around the Audra Mercantile, built by her parents, Meno and Julia Hunt in 1912. She has a story for every family possession in the store.*

*The Audra Mercantile is located in Bradshaw, a small community south of Abilene. The town was once a thriving cotton ginning stop on the Abilene and Southern Railroad.*

can see, almost as clearly as Opal can, Meno on one side of the store, selling chickens, eggs, cream, sacks of meal and sugar, plow points and brooms, and Julia on the other side, measuring out fabric, selling lace, buttons, shoes, hats.

"I'll bet you don't know what this is!" Opal begins a kind of game which she will play with me in open delight at my not knowing most of the answers. I'm baffled, but Opal explains: "You put the charcoal in the bottom and your iron on the rack. It's a charcoal iron warmer!" Her face lights up, either at my not knowing or at my understanding, I'm not sure which.

She turns quickly and gestures. "Mama's stove! A 'New Perfection,' heated with kerosene, see? I still cook with kerosene — cut my own wood, too!"

I know about early stoves, but on the next item, I fail again. She helps me. "It's a fireless cooker. See, it has this round stone in the bottom. It was heated on the stove like an iron. Mama cooked beans in it overnight." I can see Julia Hunt in Opal's eyes.

Another unfamiliar apparatus: "Mama's steamer — for fruit cakes and canning." Opal smiles again, her face like an open fan. "Here's something else you won't know." She is right. I don't. "It's a wash boiler. You set it on the stove and it boils your clothes clean. I've seen Mama use that a hundred times!" I've never seen anyone so happy in remembering.

We move to one of the old glass counters, filled with more of her family treasures. Here, heavily bound ledgers, scuffed and worn, written in Meno Hunt's Spencerian hand, list groceries sold on credit to cotton farmers. Opal touches them gently, then picks up a yellowed box of pin points, perhaps the same kind Meno used to write in his ledgers. Memory flutters in my own mind: A tight-lipped teacher, standing and demonstrating in the air before a class of nervous young pupils. "Roll, roll, roll, swing!" Over and over, repeating and gesturing, as I tried to copy the perfect Palmer script displayed on the cards above the blackboard. My palms grow damp again, remembering.

"Over here was the dry goods section." I realize Opal has darted across the store without my knowing it. "Do you know what these are?" She is pointing to a round display stand with long metal hooks hanging from it, a button at the end of each hook. A memory flashes again, and suddenly I see a small pair of high-top, black patent shoes — with buttons.

"Button hooks!" I almost shout, happy that at last I have a correct answer.

She picks up a shallow box. "Do you know what these are?" She is delighted with anticipation of my reaction. I'm a little stunned but even more curious about what I see in the box. Rattlesnake rattlers.

"Right! I collect them. Killed me one of my own right over there inside the front door. Didn't know it was a rattler till I came back with the hoe." She is matter-of-fact.

It is June, and the store has no fan and little circulation. Only the high, tin ceiling provides room for the heat to rise in the big store. I think of Julia Hunt in the photograph on the wall, dressed in a long, black skirt. How did she stand the summers? I look around at her washboard, her kerosene stove, her dishes. I have to ask, even though I already know the answer. "Are any of these beautiful old things for sale?"

Opal is quick to answer. "Of course not! It would be like selling my life!" I understand.

She remembers I don't know about her cats. Their pictures are tacked to the wall near her rocking chair. "That's Mona and that's Lisa. Lisa was my favorite cat, and she died on Palm Sunday. But my prayers were answered. She was seventeen years old and was so thin. My prayer was she'd go easy, and I was on the bed with her when she gasped and died. I said, 'I couldn't cross Jordan with her, but I did go to the banks with her.'"

Opal never married, and she loves to tell jokes, referring to herself as "the old maid." Sitting in her rocking chair under the faded, red buggy robe used by her parents, she recites an epitaph she says her brother wrote:

Here lie the bones of Samantha Jones,
To her life was no terror,
Born a maid, died a maid,
No hits, no runs, no errors!

She laughs, and so do I. Is that what she would like written on her tombstone? No, she has a better idea. "Don't you put 'Miss' on my tombstone. Like the old maid said, 'I haven't missed nearly as much as folks think I have!'" She laughs some more and rocks harder.

She grows serious. "Do you know I'm perfectly satisfied with what I've got?" I hadn't doubted it for a minute. "I like to say 'I ain't got nothin' I don't want, and I don't want nothin' I ain't got.'"

Before I leave, she wants to sing her "theme song" for me. She rocks and sings, "I wish I was a little rock, a-sitting on a hill, doing nothing all the day but just a-sitting still. I wouldn't eat, I wouldn't sleep, I wouldn't even wash but just sit still a thousand years and rest myself, begosh!" She laughs, then adds, "Sometimes when I'm in a good singing mood, I just tear around in here and sing my song!"

As I leave Opal in the Audra Mercantile Store with her song and her memories, I think I have just met a truly contented woman. I think of her answer to my question about closing the store. "If I was through with it, it'd be closed tomorrow."

Of course I know she is right.

6

# Camp Verde General Store and Post Office

*Today's general store overflows with country crafts, home-made bonnets, beef jerky, books on Texas, and everything from wind chimes to wall plaques with the camel motif.*

*The camel experiment in Texas proved impractical.*
— Historical marker, Camp Verde

CAMP VERDE  Before you ever set foot in the Camp Verde General Store and Post Office south of Kerrville, you need to learn about the camels because once inside, you are going to wonder. You should also know that the original Williams Community Store on the same site was built in 1857 but was swept away by a flood around the turn of the century. Today's two-story stone building was finished only six months after the flood, so it holds a lot of history within its walls.

Back to the camels. In 1854 Jefferson Davis was secretary of war under President Franklin Pierce, who still had memories of the Mexican War a decade earlier. He remembered how useless in the rough, arid southwestern country were the army mules and their wagons. Thus he conceived the idea of importing camels from the Middle East. The following year a congressional bill was passed, approving the idea.

A total of 120 camels were imported in three shiploads and landed near Indianola on the Texas coast. Disbelieving onlookers chuckled, then watched with wonder as the camels ambled easily across the sandy beach.

In August of 1856 the first load of camels arrived at Fort Camp Verde, the chosen site of the camel experiment. Maj. Henry C. Wayne had built an authentic caravanserai, faithfully modeled to the scale and height of the camels' native Arabia. Army troopers were amused and unconvinced until they quickly learned that the camels could saunter over rough terrain, through rain and mud, could eat prickly pear cacti and thorny grasses, and could travel days without water. Camel-borne light artillery could go anywhere an Indian could.

At the outbreak of the Civil War in 1861, the fort passed into the hand of the Confederacy with Jefferson Davis as president. During the war, Texas Confederates used some of the camels to carry cotton to Brownsville and Mexico to swap for vital supplies. In 1865 the fort was taken over by the government and abandoned in 1869.

After the war, the camels were either sold or released, some later to be seen roaming free in Arizona, California, and Mexico. A photograph of New Braunfels in the early 1900s shows at least two camels in a circus parade, perhaps some of the descendants of the first ones in Texas. A 1910 fire destroyed the fort's buildings, and today its only remains are part of a private ranch.

Inside the Camp Verde General Store and Post Office, the visitor who knows about the camels is not surprised to see the camel motif on everything from wall plaques to wind chimes. The store is literally overflowing with things to buy: country crafts (many by Hill Country artists), dolls, homemade bonnets, paintings, raw honey, rat cheese cut from an antique cheese block, pickled eggs, Kerrville beef jerky, and preserves. It is a souvenir hunter's paradise. The store also carries a good line of books on Texas subjects and a catalog of their gifts available by mail.

The old tin ceiling and antiques for sale seem more appropriate than the modern gifts, and the most interesting items for many visitors are — naturally — not for sale. An 1875 candy case holds fresh candies. You can admire never-worn baby shoes inside an antique glass case; an old hatbox for a man's fine beaver hat; ladies' turn-of-the-century, white kid shoes; old medicines to help or cure almost any ailment of the day; and a porcelain, bottle-shaped bedwarmer. A time-burnished wooden Indian guards the old post office boxes in continuous use since 1887. Look up through the pressed tin ceiling and you see how part of the original upstairs floor has been cut away so that you see the gifts also overflowing that part of the store.

Outside, in the shaded patio, you can contemplate the life of the store and post office which continued to serve pioneer ranchers long after the fort was closed and the camels were gone. In the past, silent movies were shown on the white walls outside. Now you are surrounded by stone sculpture, bird baths, and — not surprisingly — a large, leafy camel topiary.

Across the road from the store on Verde Creek is a beautiful little roadside park. Beside it, a granite historical marker concludes that the camel experiment there "proved impractical." Don't you believe it.

# 5 | P. Lesser and Son — General Merchandise

*LBJ came in one day when he was campaigning for some office . . . and wanted to know what kind of hats the farmers around here wear.*

— Harry Lesser

CHAPPELL HILL  Any time except bluebonnet season, the Fourth of July, or during the October Scarecrow Festival, Chappell Hill fine-tunes its picture of a quiet, historic little town. Drive onto long, wide Main Street on an early summer morning and find a black dog sleeping on the walk in front of an old storefront. On the curb, George Simpson sits, talking with a friend before meandering off down the street to his job at the Stage Coach Inn. No other cars nor people, but someone has turned on a garden hose to water the shrubbery in front of the bank, its gurgle about the only sound to be heard.

Early morning is a good time to read all the signs and historical markers along the street. The fire truck fund thermometer is registering $15,000 toward the $25,000 goal; Bernice Shaver's drug store serves eight flavors of Blue Bell ice cream; the white frame Methodist church was rebuilt in 1900 after the fire; merchant John E. Glass built the Old Rock Store in 1869; "This Way" to the 1893 Circulating Library; and "P. Lesser & Son — General Mdse." sells smoked country sausage, fresh eggs, homemade dill pickles, hoop cheese, and tomato relish.

Around 8:30, a big sedan drives up and parks in front of P. Lesser & Son, and nonagenarian Harry Lesser gets out. A business day on Chappel Hill's Main Street has begun.

Judge Lesser, the oldest justice of the peace in the state, arrives early every day at the store, now run by son Phil. Harry's father Phillip Lesser built

*In Chappell Hill, Harry Lesser still oversees the store his parents built at the turn of the century.*

the front portion of the store before 1905 and added the back section in 1911. Harry was born in his parents' home behind the store in 1894.

Before settling down to his J.P. duties for the day, Harry invites me to walk around the store while he relates its history. He walks slowly but erectly, aided a bit by a cane, and wearing a long-sleeved white shirt and tie even though the day promises more record heat. Phil joins us and occasionally adds store trivia, eager to share his heritage from P. Lesser and his son.

Here and there, the floor's warps and waves rise unexpectedly. The heavy black safe that once belonged to Dr. W. L. Weems rests solidly on two planks, but if the water in the lake scene painted on its door were real, it would run right out the Lessers' back door.

Iron bars block the back door opening that looks

*Lesser's son Phil runs the store while his dad (above) attends to duties as the oldest justice of the peace in the state. His office is a desk at the back of the store.*

out on the spot where Harry's father had his buggy shed and horse stall. On the inside door, penciled on cardboard, I read fading notations, a record of Harry's cattle breeding: "Heifer calf born Feb. 2, 1947. Today bred old Jersey Heifer." Harry chuckles at my city-bred interest. The obsolete kerosene pump stands inside the door, last used how many years ago? I forget to ask but am sure Harry would know exactly.

Phil wants me to taste their cheese. It is good. Near the cheese counter on an old table, jars of local honey sit in rows on a red-and-white checked oilcloth cover. I want to see their big selection of men's straw hats across the room, and Harry wants to tell me a story about Lyndon Johnson and a hat.

"LBJ came in one day when he was campaigning for some office — way back — and wanted to know what kind of hats the farmers around here wear. I told him, and he took off his fifty-dollar Stetson, asked me to keep it for him, then he bought one of my farmer hats and left to go out in the fields. When he returned, I gave him his Stetson back and asked him what he was going to do with the straw hat he bought. He said, 'I'm going to throw it out the window when I leave town.'"

The Washington County clerk comes into the store and goes to the "office" at the back. For the rest of the day he will answer the telephone, do paperwork, and occasionally step over to the counter to sell some hoop cheese. Pretty soon he is joined by the highway patrol officer who also catches up on some paperwork at the desk next to Harry's (but he doesn't sell cheese).

I learn that U.S. 290 is not the place to be careless about your driving speed, driving without a license, or not wearing your seatbelt. "We sometimes process as many as forty tickets a day," Harry tells me. Ignorance of the law is no excuse either. Some Japanese tourists who did not understand about the U.S. speed limit drove through too fast and told Harry, "We drive as fast as we want to in Japan." He only fined them ten dollars.

Harry bought the twenty-fifth car in the county in 1925, a five-passenger Dodge touring car. His instructor had a little trouble teaching him to drive and said, "You're too used to driving a wagon or a buggy. If we could take the fenders off so you could see the wheels, you wouldn't have so much trouble."

Back then, P. Lesser and Son still sold a lot of axle grease. Harry remembers other things — Octagon soap, Snapp tobacco, and brooms hanging from the ceiling broom rack as they still do. He remembers his father asking Will Taylor, who ran the icehouse, what he did with all that money he made selling ice. Will said, "I buy more ice."

"That's pretty much what you do in this business, too," Harry observes. "You take money you get selling groceries, and you buy more groceries."

You can buy just about any modern grocery item in Lesser's store today — except beer. "I tell people they've come to one of three businesses in town that don't sell beer," Harry says. "The other places you can't buy beer are the post office and the bank."

Today you can't buy axle grease in the store either, but you can get a woodstove, stove pipe, and a coal oil lamp.

On one of the ceiling posts, an old poem by Rachel Field entitled "General Store" describes the stores of days gone by but also, in a way, P. Lesser and Son today.

> Someday I'm going to have a store
> With a tinkly bell hung over the door,
> With real glass cases and counters wide
> And drawers all spilly with things inside.
> There'll be a little of everything:
> Bolts of calico, balls of string,
> Jars of peppermint, tins of tea,
> Pots and kettles and crockery,
> Seeds in packets, scissors bright,
> Kegs of sugar, brown and white,
> Sarsaparilla for picnic lunches,
> Bananas and rubber boots in bunches,
> I'll fix each window and dust each shelf
> And take the money in all myself.

9

It will be my store and I will say,
"What can I do for you today?"

Harry and Phil want to make sure I see everything I came to see. In between waiting on customers and introducing me to friendly townspeople, they show me some store calendars with photographs of old Chappel Hill scenes, even one with a baby picture of Harry. They want to be sure I see the rest of their town with all the buildings bearing historic medallions and listed on the National Register of Historic Places — like the Waverly and Browning plantations, and the community hall in the Old Rock Store with its "hanging." This turns out to be a spectacular six-by-thirty-foot folk stitchery depicting the town's history, created by women in the Chappell Hill Historical Society.

When I leave the store and walk out on the big front porch, I notice that the sleeping black dog across the street is still asleep. Of course he can't know that the best part about this little town and its general store is that whenever he wakes up, everything will be almost exactly the same.

# 6 | Cherokee Grocery Store

*Everyone you meet in Cherokee wants you to stay a while longer and meet someone who will be glad to tell you about the "good old days."*

CHEROKEE   Most people will agree that the "good old days" weren't all that good, and in many ways they are right, but in Cherokee in San Saba County, a real part of the good old days is still the ordinary way of life.

"Some of the kids move away, even though a lot of them don't want to, but then they come back," says Sue Rhoades, co-owner of the Cherokee Grocery Store along with her husband Herman. Hang around Cherokee for only an hour or so, and you will understand how the kids feel.

In this little town, caring about your neighbor is an everyday kind of attitude with all of the 200 or so residents. Take the grocery store. When you step inside, one of the first things to catch your eye will be the old scales on the counter by the cash register. The trademark on the front reads "Made by the Standard Computing Company, Detroit, Michigan, 1909." But more than a means of weighing customers' meats and vegetables, the scales provide a kind of community bulletin board. Taped to the front is an up-to-date list of Cherokee's sick persons hospitalized in Llano, San Antonio, and Houston. When there is a death, the notice informs everyone and tells which home to take food prepared for the family funeral gathering. If a fire breaks out in town or nearby, someone calls the store, and Sue or Herman will telephone all the volunteer firemen.

Many Cherokee citizens subscribe to the *Austin American-Statesman* and pay for their subscriptions by mail. They pay two additional dollars per month to Sue and Herman for driving to Llano for the papers every day of the week. Subscribers pick up their papers from a convenient stack in front of the store.

*In Cherokee, caring about one's neighbor is an everyday attitude among the 200 or so residents. In the store, notices of deaths, illnesses, and other announcements are taped to the cash register so everyone can see.*

Does anyone who is not a subscriber ever take a paper? Sue showed surprise when she said she did not think so. I was ashamed for asking.

Some of the store's merchandise is kept inside an antique display case with glass sides and a curved glass top. (Like the scales, it is not for sale.) In order to wander through the narrow aisles, you will have to step around fragrant bushel baskets of just-picked squash, tomatoes, green beans, cucumbers, and, in the fall, pecans. They will be stacked on the old oak floor right in front of the big box of fresh turkey eggs.

What you can't possibly miss — and wouldn't want to — is the enormous oak refrigerator, originally an icebox cooled with huge blocks of ice before it was installed with "a good Frigidaire motor." No one remembers exactly when. The multiple square doors open to an interior large enough to hold the store's entire supply of dairy products and other foods that need cooling. Sue says she can't count the number of offers they have had from people wanting to buy it. One Frigidaire salesman offered to replace it with a brand new commercial refrigerator — on an even trade. No deal.

While Sue or Herman is busy behind the meat counter, hand-slicing bacon or lunch meat, a local customer may walk in, reach behind the cash register to the stacks of cigarettes, take a pack, then nod to Sue and walk out. The nod is all he needs to get his purchase recorded on his charge account. No request for driver's license nor credit card. As in many of these small-town stores, the charge accounts are kept on simple receipt pads with the customers' names printed in large ink letters across the tops. The pads are stored upright in a cardboard box by the cash register. Some of the stores have the original metal accounts boxes, but, as in other places, Cherokee's store owners find the cardboard box works just fine.

An old clock on the wall catches my eye. Is it for sale, perhaps? Yes, a man in town fixes old clocks and sells them. Beside it, a beautiful framed photograph of a century-old log building in a leafy setting. It, too, is for sale. A local photographer just happens by while I am admiring his work. He wants to direct me to the spot, which he does, and later I am able to stop along a dusty back road and view the collapsing home — or barn? — for myself.

Everyone in Cherokee, apparently, is more than willing to talk about the town's history or suggest someone who can "tell you the whole story." Lots of Kuykendalls built the town, and a few of them are still around. Almost everyone knows about the first location of the town, on what was then known as Marble — or Mineral — Creek. On Christmas Day in 1839, there was a fierce fight between some soldiers and some Cherokee Indians. Afterwards, the creek was renamed. Then, in 1878, another fight, this one between a local family of brothers and two other men who were just passing through, proved so grisly — and fatal to several of the men — that the whole town was moved to its present location.

David Seth Hanna laid out the town, which is not far from the south side of the creek. James Samuel Hart bought the first lot and built a store. The post office was moved to Hart's store in July of 1879, and thus the town of Cherokee was born. The post office is the second oldest in San Saba County, so it is little wonder that Cherokee residents like to talk about their history. The town even had a junior college known as the West Texas Normal and Business College, which drew students from all over the state. After it burned down, it was never rebuilt, but you can see where it stood and read its historical marker.

The bank closed in 1924. The town's two doctors moved away long ago. Johnson Kuykendall's confectionary store stands, barely, a sad little building with almost no paint left on it, a few doors down from the Cherokee store. Johnson remembers exactly where all the other stores on Main Street were located: the variety store, several other grocery stores, one which also carried dry goods. He speaks with pride of Cherokee's school system today, grades one through twelve, and of their students who "go on to good jobs all over the country." He, too, knows a little about the town when it was located down the road on Cherokee Creek. Of course, that was before this "new" grocery store was built — in 1893.

Everyone you meet in Cherokee wants you to stay a while longer and meet someone who will be glad to tell you about "the good old days." Life in the town's past must have been every bit as good as these friendly people describe it, even with Indians around, but the present isn't bad either.

# 7   Peter Ingenhuett's Store

*We live on in our children. That is our only immortality.*

COMFORT   When nineteen-year-old Peter Joseph Ingenhuett arrived in Texas in 1852, he knew he was not cut out to be a farmer any more than the rest of his "freethinker" friends who had left their native Germany to escape political and religious pressures. But farming was all he could do until he could get established and put his real talents to work.

Peter may have heard indirectly about this beautiful "hill country" part of Texas from Prince Carl of Solms-Braunfels in Germany. The prince had abandoned his Texas settlement and returned home soon after New Braunfels was founded. Peter may also have heard about Fredericksburg to the northwest of New Braunfels. In both settlements, by the early 1850s, the German craftsmen pioneers were already cutting lacy, wooden "gingerbread" to adorn the outsides of their buildings and shaping handsome furniture to fill them.

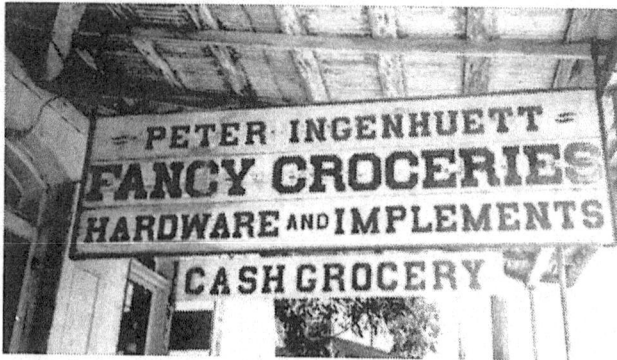

*Among the Germans who settled in Comfort, Peter Ingenhuett built a handsome limestone store on High Street that has been operating since around 1800.*

Peter's new home, which would soon be named Comfort, was laid out on land that had belonged to John Vles of New Orleans. Vles had instructed an employee, Ernest Altgelt, to dispose of the land as he chose. When Altgelt saw the beautiful little valley,

*The store was designed by San Antonio architect Alfred Giles who also designed businesses in Comfort for the Ingenhuett sons.*

*Today, the store is run by Peter's great-granddaughter, Gladys Ingenhuett Krauter. While the store sells modern-day merchandise, Comfort history shines out of every corner.*

he immediately surveyed it and divided it into town lots. By September of 1854, the town was officially established, and in 1867, Peter Ingenhuett gave up farming to become a merchant.

He built his first store that year near his homestead cottage on the south side of High Street. It did not take townspeople long to learn that Cypress Creek near the original Main Street one block away could rise dangerously during a heavy rain (a fact they would recognize again in 1870, 1900, 1932, and 1978), but the flood waters never reached the business district of High Street.

During the middle 1860s, talk around the store must have often focused on the tragedy a few years before that touched many local families. It began with the community's quarrels with the Confederacy. The German settlers' small farms had no use for slaves, nor did they believe in anyone owning them. In addition to this, they owed their new homes to the United States and refused to sign oaths of allegiance to the Confederacy. Although they had organized under the name of the Union Loyal League, they did not, as the Confederate troops suspected, plan any sort of rebellion.

In August of 1862, about sixty young men from Comfort and surrounding counties headed south to join Union forces in Mexico. They had reached the Nueces River and were camping for the night when Confederate cavalry attacked just before dawn on August 10. The young Germans were severely outnumbered, and thirty-seven of them were killed and left mutilated on the field. A few escaped to Mexico, and a few made it back to their homes.

In 1865 family and friends of the victims traveled to the battlefield and returned the bones of their loved ones to a common grave in Comfort, marked by a limestone monument bearing the words *"Treue der Union"* ("Loyalty to the Union"). Some of these survivors must have shared their tragic experiences later with other townspeople, perhaps around Peter Ingenhuett's stove in his mercantile store.

Hard work was a requirement for survival and growth in any frontier town, but at least in Comfort, religion was not. No church was built in the town until 1892, forty years after the first settlers began arriving. Nor were Bibles to be found in homes. At funeral services, sentimental German ballads were sung, not hymns. No prayers were said, and no mention of immortality was made because these Germans did not believe in it. The message was simply: "We live on in our children. That is our only immortality." When the first church was finally built, businessmen contributed with the understanding that "we not be pressured to attend." After all, that is one of the reasons they left Germany.

The number of mercantile stores built during Comfort's early years reflects the growth of the town. Names such as Schwethlem, Goldbeck, Holekamp, Osche, and Faltin became stamped on the town's history. August Faltin hired the British-born, San Antonio architect Alfred Giles to erect his new store on Main Street, one of the town's first limestone buildings.

In 1869 Peter Ingenhuett became postmaster, a position he would hold for more than twenty-five years. The post office was located in his store. He was a well-established merchant when he married young Marie Karger in 1871. Peter was thirty-eight, and Marie was eighteen. Around 1900, he hired Giles to design his own handsome new store. By then, mule-drawn wagons hauling huge limestone blocks through Comfort's wide streets had become a common sight.

Built in the middle of the 800 block of the south side of High Street, the new store was adorned in front with an ornate pediment and a cutout balcony of Bavarian design. The front door was made by Christel Lindemann, Comfort's undertaker, who was also a skilled carpenter. The porch and shutters were painted black and white, and wooden hitching posts were spaced at intervals along the street in front. The store had a basement, freight elevator, and an outside staircase. Toward the end of the 1880s, Peter added a one-story extension and removed the balcony.

He and Marie lived on the second floor above the store for a few years until they moved into the large, two-story home down the block in front of Peter's original homestead. By the turn of the century, the Ingenhuett family would own more than two-thirds of the block bounded by High, Main, and Eighth streets.

Four boys and two girls were born to Peter and Marie, and Peter wasted no time in building limestone businesses for the boys: next door to the store a saloon and dance hall for Hubert, and close by, the eight-room hotel for Ernest who operated it for about ten years. Later, the hotel was bought by Louis and Matilda Faust.

Peter's sons continued in their father's tradition. In 1890 Paul and his brother-in-law Carl Karger built a solid, limestone opera house behind the store. There, both local and traveling performers entertained townspeople who also came to the Ingenhuett-Real Halle for all-night dances. In a large, wooden gazebo between the opera house and the store, male guests could visit and drink beer. Paul also built the post office in the 800 block of High Street.

For a town composed of immigrants who brought with them to their new home not carpenters' tools but musical instruments and books, the residents adapted well to the necessities at hand. More building was done during the first twenty-five years of Comfort's existence than has been done since. Their cypress timber, *fachwerk*, and limestone buildings still stand, lovingly cared for by their descendants. High Street's 800 block may be the longest-standing, still-active business district in Texas. In 1979 a large part of the original 1854 townsite was listed in the National Register of Historic Places.

Walk under the Ingenhuett Store sign today that reads "PETER INGENHUETT ★ ★ FANCY GROCERIES ★ ★ HARDWARE AND IMPLEMENTS ★ ★ CASH GROCERY," and you may be greeted by his great-granddaughter, Gladys Ingenhuett Krauter. She and her husband Jimmy are the present owners. Here, as everywhere in Comfort, history shines out of every corner. The one-story, "new" part of the store is stocked with modern-day groceries, but step into the old part for an idea of what the store was like when Peter ran it and later son Paul, then his son Peter, Gladys's father. Try to ignore the shelves stocked with aluminum saucepans, dog collars, and garden tools, and let your eyes find the kinds of things people bought there before the hitching posts out front were removed.

Hardware — look closely, yes, those are doorknobs and hinges much like the ones used in the stores. Someone still manufactures them, and the store sells them, often to people restoring an old Comfort house. No caskets here, but there are casket handles. The prices are higher, but you can still buy the same kinds of cow, sheep, and turkey bells that the store has sold for more than a century.

Need a 1920 De Laval cream separator? Maybe not, but how about some of Dr. LeGear's prescriptions for livestock, poultry, and dogs — "satisfaction guaranteed"? Ammunition? Above the shelves where it is stocked, see one of the bullet-hole pictures made by Winchester rifle promoter Adolph Toepperwein. He left his trademark in many of the stores he visited with his wife "Plinkie" before he joined Buffalo Bill's wild west show.

You may remember when stores gave dishes or other tokens of appreciation to customers. In a case of store memorabilia, a little handpainted plate displays Ingenhuett's name. Printed on it is a painting of a brook and the Tennyson rhyme: "I chatter, chatter as I go, to join the brimming river, for men may come and men may go, but I go on forever."

Other reminders of the store's age: floor-to-ceiling ladders to roll alongside aisles to reach merchandise on high shelves; old McCaskey files on Peter's desk.

What was the funeral message before there were churches in Comfort? "We live on in our children. That is our only immortality." Gladys Ingenhuett has proudly shown me her great-grandfather's store and tells me that her son is interested in preserving it, too. Outside, on the wide, quiet 800 block of High Street, I look around at all of Peter Ingenhuett's buildings, still in use, and I think that he and his countrymen may have been right.

## 8 | Myrt's Store

*Some of the old folks bought what was left in it — pure kerosene — no lead in it.*

— Sylvia Bolton

DIALVILLE   Learning the whole story about the past of some general stores and the towns where they once flourished is not always simple. It depends on who is telling the story.

Talk to the present owner of Myrt's Store in Dialville, Sylvia Bolton, who restored it with husband Wayne, and she will tell you all she has learned since opening the store in the fall of 1985. She will describe the town when it was a lot bigger — more businesses, a hotel, a box factory, cotton gin, and tomato-packing sheds all along the railroad tracks across the road. Their store was first a drug store, built around 1908 by Acker and Halbert, then owned by Dr. Moore, who used the back room for his office. The last owner was Myrtle V. Payne, who ran a general merchandise store in the building and served as the town's telephone operator. The two-story bank next door stayed busy, and the road out front was filled, first with horses and wagons, then with automobiles heading north to Jacksonville or south to connect with the road to Palestine and Rusk.

What happened to the town? All that remains now in the thickly wooded setting is the bank, housing a Baptist mission, two churches, the store, shells of a few other buildings, and a scattering of old homes. Dr. Moore's once-handsome yellow house sits faded and neglected down the road.

Main and Caledonia streets are narrow, dirt roads leading steeply uphill through overgrowth where homes and businesses once stood. The depot and big water tank are gone. Of the sycamores that shaded the storefronts, one lonely survivor stands near the remains of the well. On a busy day, the two benches out on the sidewalk may have two people sitting on them under the rusty-red awning.

Talk with one longtime resident, and he will tell you what happened to the town. True, the tomato and cotton crops declined, the highway just missed the town by two miles, the Dialville bank merged

*Benches outside the early stores often featured advertisements by bakeries and funeral homes. Here, townspeople met to exchange news and announce personal plans.*

with the bank in Jacksonville, and the Depression years took their toll, but the town's first step into ghost towndom came with the fire.

In 1929 the hotel on the back of the corner lot at Main and Front streets burned to the ground under

*Myrt's Store in Dialville is about all that remains of the businesses that fronted the railroad track in this little East Texas town.*

14

circumstances known to everyone in town. Almost every business was destroyed. The post office did not catch fire at first but simply exploded with the heat. People in Frankston, over twenty miles away to the north, saw the smoke.

To learn more, you need to sit near the front door in one of the rickety chairs at the domino table. It may take a while. Life moves slowly in Dialville — even for East Texas. Townspeople drop in for groceries; lost tourists stick their heads in the door and ask, "Where are we?"

You learn that Confederate veteran John J. Dial from Georgia joined sixty wagons of settlers heading for Texas in 1866. This region had been settled as early as 1845. It already had a Baptist church and a cemetery. Dial farmed for a while, then opened a store. When the Kansas and Gulf Short Line Railroad came through, he deeded eight acres of land to the railroad, which laid out the town in lots. The post office was established in 1885, and the settlement was named Dialville.

During the early years, other general mercantile and grocery stores were run by John T. Bailey, J. A. Whitaker, G. W. Wallace, Tommy Fulton, Miller and Meazles, the Odoms, W. F. Jones, and C. C. Slover. C. D. Jarratt encouraged farmers to plant peach orchards and tomatoes, and soon the loading platforms by the railroad tracks were filled with crops being shipped off to market.

A big year was 1913, with the building of a theater, a second restaurant, a shoe repair shop, and the establishment of a newspaper. That year the Dialville Brass Band was organized and became a great source of pride for the town.

While you listen to townsfolk about Dialville's past, Sylvia may be at the back of the store, making lunch sandwiches for young laborers who were born in the town or arranging bright-red, fresh tomatoes in the old tin bowl she found in the store. Above her head on upper shelves sit other odds and ends she has found — old soda pop bottles, rusted coffee cans, farm tools, heavy wooden shipping boxes, and a VC Fertilizer sign that Sylvia says "was perfectly preserved under all those layers of grease and red dirt." An elderly couple from Reklaw (Walker, spelled backwards) have eight dozen eggs to leave with her

this day. They buy some of her popular "rat cheese" before they leave.

Sylvia wants to tell about "Myrt's ghost." One day when she and Wayne were sitting at the front of the store, the old clock on the back wall suddenly fell forward, striking a counter before falling to the floor. They went back and examined the nail that had been holding it, still firmly in the wall. The back of the clock showed no weakness nor reason for it to fall from the nail. Sylvia says it was no doubt Myrt, letting them know she is happy her store is open again.

Sylvia says the kerosene pump was too heavy to move, so it still stands at the front of the store. "Some of the old folks bought what was left in it — pure kerosene, no lead in it." In a tattered ledger, I read some of the other things customers used to buy: a child's straw hat — 75¢; two dozen eggs — 21¢; one parasol — $1.25; ten yards of calico — 70¢; for Miss Jeanne Douglas, slippers — $2.25, hat — 50¢. The store also sold lamp wicks, coal oil (from the faded red pump), pocketknives, snuff, and salt in cotton bags. A paper sack, from perhaps the store's later years, reads "W. A. Odom — General Merchandise — Dry Goods, Groceries & Feed — Auto Accessories, Gas & Oil."

Traveling drummers made regular calls on stores located in towns served by a railroad. If a town had a hotel, it attracted even more of the salesmen, and Dialville had both. One resident remembers that they often carried such modern conveniences as eyeglasses.

Sylvia's husband Wayne grew up in Dialville, and their son Marc is helping to refurbish the store and the other buildings they now own. Marc's grandmother still lives nearby. He will be happy to tell you about the "Dialville Plunge" where the young people used to dance over by the lake.

It is a nice little town to explore, even if there isn't much to see any more. But read the historical marker by the store and visit the Rocky Springs Missionary Baptist Church with its cemetery on the hill. Then sit inside the store at the domino table and listen to the breeze in the sycamore tree. You will understand why those early residents loved it so much.

# 9 | The Northington Store

*The store in Egypt, west of Houston, still belongs to the Northington family who were among the town's earliest settlers. Today it is called John's Country Store and run by Johnny Parker.*

*Things the family didn't want . . . they just put in the store.*

— Anita Northington

EGYPT   All of the early general stores owe their lifetimes to the settlements in which they were first built, but none belongs to its founders and their descendants more than the Northington Store in Egypt, west of Houston. Currently known as John's Country Store and run by Johnny Parker, the two store buildings remain in the Northington family, whose forebears were among Egypt's earliest colonists.

This high ground above the Colorado River in Wharton County was chosen by Stephen F. Austin in 1824 as the destination for his first colony of 300 settlers. Among them was John C. Clark, who cleared and planted fifteen acres of corn in 1827. Other settlers had also brought with them from eastern states seed corn to plant in their new homes. However, the 1827 drought took a heavy toll, and rain fell only on Clark's small portion of land. Those who lost their crops came to Clark for grain to plant a new crop, and thus the phrase "going down to Egypt for corn" from the Bible passage became the source of Egypt's name.

At that time, Egypt was at the crossroads where the dirt road between Columbus to the north and

Matagorda on the Gulf Coast intersected the wagon trail from Richmond to Texana. Today, the settlement can be located on a map ten miles north of Wharton and about thirteen miles south of Eagle Lake.

One of the earliest families to settle in Egypt were the Mercers from Mississippi. Eli Mercer, nephew of Eli Whitney, built the first Egypt cotton gin in 1836 and also developed a process for making white cane sugar from the abundant cane that grew in the river. His friend and brother-in-law Gail Borden spent three years in Egypt in the early 1830s, surveying for Stephen F. Austin before moving his family to Galveston. Borden would spend many frustrating years inventing things that were never accepted before his condensed milk became a popular staple on the shelves of general stores in Egypt and throughout the country.

By 1839, Maj. Andrew Northington had started one of the first stage lines linking Egypt with Houston and Richmond. Northington and Green Cameron Duncan had Egypt's first sizeable general store in the center of the community, beginning in 1881. This store supplied the needs as well as some luxuries for the area until 1900, when Northington bought out Duncan and built the present white, frame store on Egypt's main street. Today, the first store's gray, wooden skeleton stands like a lonely onlooker, largely ignored by all but the visitor.

Northington's son, Mentor, married Elizabeth Heard, daughter of William Jones Eliott Heard, a Tennessean who arrived from Alabama with Austin's third group of colonists. John C. Clark sold half of his original league of land, about 2,000 acres, to Heard. Northington and Heard built most of the grander homes in Egypt, including the home known as Egypt Plantation. Heard fashioned the classic Georgian structure with pink brick made by slaves from the banks of nearby Caney Creek. The house was finished in 1849 and has been lived in by members of the Northington families ever since.

In 1909 Mentor Northington added a brick building to the frame store, and it contained the meat market for thirty years. It is empty today, but owner John Northington may refurbish it to serve as a museum.

The store as it was in Egypt's early life can best be seen inside the Egypt Plantation home and the depot museum which John's mother, Anita Northington, opens to tour groups. Anita also likes to show the museum of her husband, the late George Northington III, housed in the old Santa Fe Railroad depot that his father had moved to its location behind the home.

In both the home and the museum, items that were once a part of the store catch your eye. The "keeping room" is a large family room filled with treasures, many from the store. A gleaming black-and-gold sign advertises Clark's sewing thread. The coffee table is actually a big, framed picture of some dogs, and in the dining room hangs a chandelier that once hung in the meat market. Anita explains that "things the family didn't want or were tired of, they just put in the store." Visitors are grateful that apparently the family never threw anything away.

When the Cane Belt Railroad laid its tracks across the road, more and more goods from faraway places were shipped in for sale in the store. At the beginning of the 1920s, counter sales catalogs offered customers all kinds of tempting luxuries, from diamond jewelry to floor lamps, from toasters to silver-plated tea services.

The Spence Mead Company, Wholesale Tailors, showed the latest in men's suits in their catalog, and the 1920–21 Marshall Field's Chicago catalog (#321) advertised diamonds, jewelry, watches, toiletware, electric lamps, clocks, cut and colored glass, adding, "The illustrations and descriptions are accurate." One Marshall Field's catalog included a cardboard ring sizer for the shopper's convenience.

The catalog pages reveal that not all the items were as inexpensive as we might like to believe they were in the "good old days." Diamond rings and necklaces, for example, along with solid gold and sterling silver mesh ladies' purses, "Ivoirtex Toilet Ware," or imitation ivory ladies' dresser sets, were far from inexpensive.

These kinds of items, however, were not within the reach of most of the store's customers, many of whom were plantation hands and farmers. Ninety percent of them bought on credit, settling their accounts when their crops came in as did hundreds of other general store customers during this period.

Walk slowly around the store today on the original floor, under the old ceiling, and look closely to see odds and ends left over from the early years,

most of them displayed casually on the top shelf that runs almost the length of the store on both sides: grindstones; round, basketlike potato separators; a plow handle; a trunk; an early stamp machine. Inside the once-handsome office area, enclosed by dark wooden railings, two heavy desks show evidence of many hours spent by Northington men, working on store records. Behind the office, wooden hardware bins line the wall near the "not-for-sale" octagonal hardware cabinet.

On the floor, heavy table counters hold modern groceries as do the original, dark-stained shelves with massive wooden drawers underneath, perhaps once used to hold piece goods. The store also sold caskets, and one old sales receipt reads "casket handles," suggesting that some were made by a local person.

In the empty meat market through the side wall door, a rusty sign recognized a longstanding business relationship: "Ten Years of Friendly Relations — G. H. Northington — Good Year Company."

On the back porch between the store and the feed storage room, the faded red kerosene pump that filled hundreds of cans sits behind its wooden lattice enclosure. Here, local products were unloaded — corn, pecans, sugar cane, and sugar.

Egypt is a quiet little rural community where the past hangs as gently as the moss on the trees. Standing half-hidden by trees, "Miss Sadie's Mansion" behind the store is a ghostly, pillared plantation home, as little noticed as the 1880s Duncan-Northington store across the road. "Miss Sadie" was the sister of George Northington, Jr., the fourth generation of Egypt Northingtons, and she lived in the house almost twenty years with her mother.

This home and others built by the family, together with the tenderly preserved Egypt Plantation and the Northington-Heard family cemetery, give a feeling of continuance to the crossroads community. Some of the graves were covered with the same pink bricks of the plantation to keep the Indians from robbing them. Their crumbling remains rest under the protective shade of the old trees, safe today from any Indians or intruders.

Stephen F. Austin and all those early Northingtons and Heards, as well as others who first settled here, would be proud.

17

*Only the post office remains in the Fischer Store today. Since 1902, a Fischer has always been postmaster, beginning with Hermann and presently Gertrude Fischer.*

*My account is not correct. I have never bought any snuff or ginger from you on time.*

— An early customer

FISCHER   Around Canyon Reservoir in Comal County, the hills are filling up with new resorts, retirement homes, boating and fishing supply stores, real estate companies, and road signs for construction. City people are eager to find ideal sites for quiet relaxation, and there is no doubt that this is a good spot for them. I almost hate to give the exact location for fear that too many more people will learn that the most restful place around was discovered back in the early 1850s by Otto and Hermann Fischer at a crossroads on Farm Road 32, a few miles southeast of Blanco.

In 1853 Hermann had 160 acres, on which he built a one-room log cabin and began raising stock. When neighbors settled nearby, he built a log store which grew from a one-wagon business to a dozen wagons drawn by six-mule teams to haul products from the community to the store. Soon the settlement, along with the post office in the store, were known officially as Fischer's Store, Texas. In 1902 Hermann Fischer built the present store, and the town is now known as Fischer, Texas. The post office has had a Fischer for postmaster since the beginning: first Hermann, then Hermann Jr., Willie, Eddie, and today, Gertrude Fischer.

Climb the three front steps of the huge, corru-

*Visitors have to squint through the shadows to see the few remaining store furnishings such as the rotating, octagonal hardware cabinet found in all the early stores.*

gated tin store, go through the big, wooden doors, and peer into the long, cool dimness. You will think someone forgot to turn the calendar pages and to restock the dusty shelves and display cases about eighty years ago. You feel you may be the first person to pass through those doors in a long time. But tucked into one corner, a single light burns inside the post office that is still operating. Close by is the massive black safe with gold block letters reading HERMAN FISCHER (only one n in Hermann here).

On a corner wall, a large, old blackboard suggests other activity around the store through the years. Neatly listed in chalk is the annual rainfall every year since 1890. One of the record years was 1957, when rainfall measured 54.54 inches; May of 1986 brought almost ten and one-half inches. The record low temperature was reached in 1962 at -8 degrees. The maximum was also recorded that year on August 9 at 2:00 P.M., when the thermometer reached 109 degrees.

As you walk around over the grayed, worn floor, you have to squint through the shadows to see the few remaining items that were once for sale. If you like, you could reach up and pull the string on one of the tin-shaded light bulbs to see the long, wooden counters, now mostly bare. Atop one, there is a rotating octagonal hardware cabinet with scores of little drawers for screws and bolts and other such things. On a shelf is an early-day radio, and by the woodstove an empty broom and mop rack. It is easy to imagine people huddled around the stove on one of those cold days recorded on the blackboard.

On shelves, piled in careless stacks, faded post office ledgers list money orders and other postal transactions. For an hour or more, I curl up in one of the wide window seats with daylight sifting through the curtain of dust on the window and poke through a dilapidated cardboard box filled with an inventory of the past.

Sales receipts from the early 1920s list: 900 tablespoons — $3.00; 900 teaspoons — $6.00; 22½ pounds of bacon at twenty-five cents a pound — $5.62; one casket — $65.00. From the Walter Tips Company, Austin, one rifle — $11.50, postage — ten cents. From Vos & Kooch Hardware, Crockery, Stoves and Cutlery, Austin, one brick buttermold — $3.25, eleven cowbells — $1.55, and eight sheep bells — $1.60. Washing machines from the Boss Washing Machine Company of Cincinnati were understandably popular with housewives.

Even earlier correspondence, before 1900, shows that Fischer did business with established Texas merchants such as Louis Henne of New Braunfels, who dealt in "Hardware, Stoves, Pumps, Tinware, Iron Roofing, Farming Implements, and Barbed Wire." A letter from H. D. Gruene from the town that was then called Goodwin Post Office, Texas, offered Fischer good prices for salt, tobacco, buckets, thread, and potatoes. Gruene's letterhead announced his dealership in "Hardware, Groceries, Dry Goods, Crockery, Wooden Ware, Etc., Etc." and "Agent for the Mitchell Wagon."

One of Fischer's dealings with a postal customer is revealed in the lines — and between the lines — of a letter to Fischer written in June of 1894.

Dear Sir,
    I am very anxious to have the enclosed letter reach Miss Annie Rogers by tomorrow (Thursday) or at latest Friday, and as she lives on the mail line half way between your office and Blanco, the only way I can get it to her in time is to send it to you and depend on your kindness to hand it at once to the mail carrier as he goes up tomorrow and he can deliver it without leaving the road. Give him the enclosed quarter for his trouble and I am sure it will get there all right. If you will do this I will see you in person the last of the week and thank you for the favor.
                                        Yours truly . . .

The letter was typewritten on the letterhead of an office supply firm in Waco.

Some of Fischer's own correspondence leaves no doubt as to his taking his business seriously. He kept scores of children's penmanship notebooks, listing the names and details of customers who owed him money. Letters to some of them stated in unmistakable terms how he felt about their debts and their payment: "I have received only $5.00 on your note so far but hope you will be able to send me some money on the note this fall as you have good — and we have bad — crops."

Replies were often equally direct:

My account is not correct. I have never bought any snuff or ginger from you on time. I am not able just now to remit. I do not think you ought to charge so much interest. If you are really needing the money, I can make some sacrifice to pay you . . . If I had not owed you, I would have moved from here long ago. If you need any hauling or freighting perhaps I can pay you some that way.

A traveler enters the store and approaches Postmaster Fischer in her little lighted cubicle behind the old mailboxes. Can he get a beer? No, they sell a few soft drinks, chips, that's all. This is government property, so no beer. The man smiles a puzzled thanks and steps back out into the daylight. He glances at the somehow anachronistic newspaper dispenser at the foot of the store steps, then walks to his car parked under the shady clump of trees at the lonely crossroads. He looks back at Fischer's Store. Perhaps he has stumbled into a kind of Twilight Zone, and he looks around as if to see if there are others there as bewildered as he is. There aren't, and he drives away down one of the dusty roads.

I refocus my eyes back into the shadowy interior of the store. It must have once been a busy place, filled with shoppers and neighbors trading news, schoolchildren from the hilltop school where Otto and Hermann Fischer served on the school board. Today, the musty emptiness makes it a lonely kind of time capsule that almost pleads for someone to reorder and stock the shelves with teaspoons and cowbells and overalls.

19

# 11   Ellis Mercantile Store

*Visitors to the Ellis Mercantile Store in Frankston need plenty of time to see everything. The Ellis family sells men's straw hats, snuff, chamber pots, coal oil lamps, overalls, groceries, woodstoves, well buckets, even crocks for making home brew.*

*Some folks don't want anyone to know they make home brew, so we just tear the label off the malt can and call it "a can of peaches."*

— Pam Ellis Murphy

FRANKSTON  For a first-time visitor, the best parts of the Ellis Mercantile Store in Frankston are the surprises. Unlike a modern supermarket where you glide smoothly down aisles lined with predictable merchandise, in the Ellis store, you can spend long minutes simply trying to identify the things pinned to "the wire."

The Ellises have strung heavy wire almost the length of the store, and above the cash register counter at the front, Clyde Ellis has hung family keepsakes, favorite sayings, and other things impossible to classify. For example, there is a photo birth announcement of his pet squirrel Sissy's "four new babies," a dried tobacco leaf, a dried flying squirrel (no relation to Sissy), shoes worn by grandsons Keith and Mike when they were much younger, and snapshots of family and friends. A child's potty chair used to hang on the wire, but Mrs. Ellis took it home.

If you need to buy a hat when you step into Ellis's to shop, you are not likely to forget it. Hanging from the wires over narrow aisles are dozens of western-style straw hats and railroader caps. Pam Ellis

Murphy, Clyde's granddaughter, says they sell more snuff and chewing tobacco than hats, "but we sell a lot of hats, too."

Ellis's sign out front says they sell "Groceries, Hardware, Feed, Dry Goods & Shoes." That doesn't quite cover it. The store's stock is a cluttered jumble of anachronisms, but it is hard to decide which ones are out of sync with the calendar. Coal oil lamps sit on shelves next to new canned goods; chamber pots rest near plastic buckets; and horse collars hang above the frozen food cooler. Shoppers can buy overalls, woodstoves, well buckets, even crocks for making home brew. Pam says "some folks don't want anyone to know they make home brew, so we just tear the label off the malt can and call it 'a can of peaches.'"

Behind the counter at the front of the store, there used to be a hole in the floor made when Clyde did not want to walk all the way to the back door to test the shotguns he was selling. "It was a real conversation piece, but it was weakening the floor, so we fixed it."

Clyde bought the store in 1952, and over the years he has had a couple of merchandising problems. One time he carried raccoons — live ones. He was selling them until he found out he had to have a license and gave up that idea. He used to put a lot of his merchandise out on the sidewalk. Then a city ordinance prohibited this kind of advertising. Clyde refused to move his display inside, though, even with the threat of a hundred-dollar fine. He told the city officials that he would not move his merchandise unless all the other merchants did. None of them budged, and the sidewalk sales continued.

At one time he carried wooden legs. When asked how many sizes he stocked, not ever knowing what he would need, he answered, "I just carried one size. It didn't matter if someone had to limp a little."

The store faces the shady town square and park, opposite the bandstand and the Frankston Depot Library and courthouse museum. The land for the park was donated in 1902 by Miss Frankie Miller, who became the town's namesake. C. P. Jones, who built the store, was one of Frankston's earliest citizens.

Other former owners included Marvin Cely and Gus Hassell. Some of their names are barely legible on the outside of the building, but Jones's name and the date he built the store are permanently recorded on the cast-iron plate at the store entrance.

In 1966 Ralph Ellis joined his father in running the store, and Ralph is carrying on all its traditions. Charge tickets are filed in a worn, wooden box near the front counter under "the wire." A man needing extra cash before his Social Security check arrives can borrow twenty dollars (yes, with interest).

What do some of the older customers remember about the store from past years? "Used to be a lot of tomato-packing sheds over by the depot," one says.

Do they remember that Cynthia Ann Parker, the white girl who was captured by Comanches and later rescued (but died of grief and starvation) was first buried in the cemetery at nearby Brushy Creek along with her baby Prairie Flower? Some do, but they would rather talk about their championship high school baseball team and Frankston's annual October homecoming parade.

You can get your chain saw sharpened at the Ellis Mercantile Store, find out who in town is in the hospital, pick up some garden seed or bedding plants, or just look around. But don't plan to hurry. There's a lot to see.

## 12 | W. L. Randall General Merchandise Store

*Never a morning goes by that people don't come and say "Where's So-and-So?"*

— "Miss Hallie" Randall

FRUITVALE   Out in front of the W. L. Randall General Merchandise Store, alongside the peeling school auditorium seats and the empty Baptist church pews, you can buy a newspaper, use the public telephone, or read the Fruitvale bulletin board, which today displays an ad for a Honda boat and a cemetery lot. However, the best source of news is still inside, where all day and every day since 1916, East Texans have been coming through the store's squeaky screen door to buy groceries, hardware, feed, and clothing and to trade news items of the day.

"Before the sun comes up and until after it goes down" — that's how owner Hallie Randall describes the store's hours. She likes to keep the same hours that Mr. Randall did from the time he opened his first store in 1910 until his death in 1963.

"Never a morning goes by," she says, "that people don't come and say 'Where's So-and-So?' Everyone knows exactly who is going to drop by."

In the winter "Miss Hallie" has coffee keeping hot on the large, black Charter Oak stove that is as old as the store. Customers sit in the big rocking chair near the cash register or on the scuffed-up bench nearby. Some of them may be her former pupils; she taught school in Fruitvale for forty-seven years. On one wall, row after row of fading photographs of long-grown pupils look out on the comings and goings in the store.

Miss Hallie is not always on hand to tend the store. Since 1970 she has been Fruitvale's mayor, and she also heads up the senior citizens' center. Two brass plaques on a wall attest to her standing in

*Every day since 1916, East Texans have been coming through the W. L. Randall squeaky screen door to buy groceries, hardware, feed, and clothing and to trade news items of the day.*

the community. One reads "Outstanding Citizen — Van Zandt County — 1974," and another, "Outstanding Senior Citizen — 1978."

Antique dealers and collectors gasp with happy disbelief when they step into the store and look around. Miss Hallie has lined the shelves above the merchandise which *is* for sale with dozens of old, family treasures which are *not*. She is used to people asking if anything is for sale. But if what you are interested in is Fruitvale and the people and the days that will never be again, she will be glad to share these with you. To see them clearly, you need to look at them through *her* eyes, *her* memory. She does not see the dust, the faded colors. In the photographs of her pupils, she sees the children as they looked each morning when they entered her classroom in the H.E. Travis School behind the store. They called her "Miss Hallie," she remembers with a smile. Looking at the rusty tobacco cutter, the milk cans, the big

*"Miss Hallie" Randall keeps the same hours her husband kept for the store — "before the sun comes up until after it goes down."*

metal scoops for beans and sugar in the drawer bins under the counter, she sees them just as they were when they were used every day in the store.

Fruitvale was never very large, she says. It is at its peak right now with about 370 people. She remembers years ago, when there were two service stations, a blacksmith shop, Dr. Hazel's drug store next door, a shop that made crossties and one that made wagon parts, a Baptist church, and a Congregational church (which later became Methodist). Over the railroad tracks in front of the store, U.S. Highway 80 was once an unpaved road leading to Dallas to the west, Longview to the east.

Farmers would buy on credit back then. She shows me one of Mr. Randall's ledgers — she calls him "Mr. Randall," too. The date is 1915, when cotton sold for fifteen cents a pound. In those days, the store had four clerks, two for each side of the store. On one side were groceries, feed, and hardware; on the other, clothing and dry goods. The cashier sat high in the center of the store behind the huge cash register, still in place. Jim Creagle had his barber shop at the back of the store, Miss Hallie tells me. His ornately carved oak barber chair now sits up front, re-covered with red velvet. Miss Hallie

touches it gently, then points to a large, framed mirror on the top shelf around the room. Creagle's mirror, she says. She looks outside and smiles. "Mr. Randall used to sell ice cream cones for a nickel right out there." I see him, too.

A man in brand-new denim overalls, boots, and a western hat comes in. Miss Hallie knows him, of course. He is a retired farmer and wants to buy some barbed wire to fix a gate. It comes out "bobbed war."

I ask about a back entrance that I noticed earlier. Miss Hallie tells me it was the post office's outside entrance, and we go back to look at the old mail boxes. A large cabinet radio stands on the floor near the door to the post office. "We always kept the radio on, right inside here, so people could pick up their mail, then come in and listen if they wanted to."

What about the old wood cookstove in the corner? Miss Hallie smiles. "Oh, that was Mama's. See the warming oven here? All of us kids would make a break for it after school to get us a sweet potato or a biscuit." Time has suddenly taken another swing backward, and we are back in Hallie's childhood. She picks up a heavy, black skillet. "This was my grandfather's. My grandmother died and he had to do all the cooking, so this really got a lot of use. He was a good cook." I see another man in denim overalls, standing by another woodstove, cooking for his children, doing what needed to be done.

Friends have given Miss Hallie some of the antiques such as the jukebox. How old? She doesn't know, but the records on it include "Dust on My Telephone" and "Rooming House Boogie," wherever that places it in hit-parade history. The gum machine on the wall next to the jukebox has been there as long as the store has been here — "Shor's Chewing Gum — One Penny — 1916."

An old phone booth houses the original telephone. "We had one of the first phones in town," she remembers. "We would take messages for people. If it was a death message, we'd try to go right away." Across the road, a Union Pacific train rattles by on tracks that were first laid in 1873. Miss Hallie looks out at the train, then takes an old lantern down from a shelf. "We used to dispatch our mail by rail, and our postmaster would use this lantern to swing back and forth — right out there — to signal the train that he had the mail bag ready."

Above the new blue jeans, western hats, and shirts on counters, my eyes sweep up to the top shelf just under the white tracery of the pressed tin ceiling. There, in a row, are dust-covered, high-topped women's shoes, two rocking chairs, a tiny child's chair, a Clark's Our New Thread cabinet, Jim Creagle's mirror, dim with dust — fragments of ordinary days in the past.

There is no dust on Miss Hallie's memory. "The

shoes were left over from stock," she explains, "but we just decided one day to bring them out. The double rocker, we called it a settee. Mr. Randall and I bought that in Marshall about 1930, right after we got married. The rockers were Mr. Randall's mother's. The little chair was given to me at Christmas when I was four years old." I do some fast arithmetic — 1911.

We walk back to the counter and cash register, used every day. Mr. Kelly, a retired locksmith, has come in and is sitting in the rocking chair near the counter. Miss Hallie tells me this is the rocker that went with the rocking settee. I take the nearby bench and begin talking with Mr. Kelly.

"The thing about Fruitvale," he says, "is if you want anything done around your house or your farm, there's always someone here who can do it." I wonder how many places can be described in such a way.

Above the cash register I notice a faded bonnet in a glass-covered frame. I know it must be even more significant than the other antiques in the store. Miss Hallie follows my gaze. "My grandmother's bonnet," she explains. "See the buttons around the back? She wore it when they lived around Canton, just south of here." Miss Hallie is almost eighty. I guess at the bonnet's age.

I glance around at all the old furniture and things I did not ask about — the lightning rods, two giant hornets' nests. More shoppers come in. The old screen door bangs shut. Mr. Kelly gets up slowly and leaves. The door squeaks and bangs again. I thank Miss Hallie for her time and hospitality and step out into the bright daylight. When I look back for a second, I see her standing behind the screen door. She is waving with one hand, using the other to dab at her eye with a handkerchief. It is a gesture I noticed several times inside the store. Now I understand.

A man in faded blue jeans drives up and gets out of his car. "Is Miss Hallie here?" he asks me.

"Oh, yes," I tell him. "She certainly is."

## 13 | Darsey's General Mercantile

*Are you ready to enter into that great spirit of brotherly love and cooperation in serving the town . . . ?*
— Newspaper article, 1924

GRAPELAND   You don't have to be around Darsey's General Merchandise Store very long to understand why it is one of Texas's oldest general stores under the same family ownership, still operating in the same location — 100 years in 1986.

The store is the place to visit if you want to see Grapeland's past and present clearly. Shoppers greet strangers as if they saw each other every day. They discuss a fellow citizen's death with sadness in their voices. Someone tells you that the town built both a hospital and a nursing home without government aid. Craftsmen drop by the store to sign up in July for the annual October Peanut Festival. Owner Charley Darsey explains that he is the third-generation Darsey to run the store and proudly shares its history.

Across wide Main Street on the grassy strip alongside the railroad tracks sits the little 1906 wooden "hoosegow," a visible reminder that Grapeland folks have always felt strongly about their town.

These attitudes go back to the town's beginning. In 1872 the Houston and Great Northern Railroad

*One of Texas's oldest general stores under the same family ownership, Darsey's General Merchandise Store in Grapeland still serves as the hearthstone of the little East Texas town.*

reached Grapeland as it stretched northward to Palestine. George Darsey had come to the area earlier from Georgia, along with other new settlers from the Carolinas, Alabama, Virginia, Mississippi, and Tennessee. In 1886 he built his first store, a frame building on the corner of Maple and Front streets, facing the railroad tracks. His sign on the store's false front read "Geo. E. Darsey — Dry Goods — Groceries &

Furniture." An 1890 photograph shows a vested Darsey on the store's front porch, holding a sample of the year's cotton crop.

The cotton gin was southwest of town, and farmers also raised corn, potatoes, sugar cane, tomatoes, peas, beans, berries, and other fruits. Mustang grapes grew wild, as they still do, and became the source of Grapeland's name.

The Darsey store carried all the things the townspeople needed and perhaps a few things they sometimes wanted more than needed. Old records show that one customer consumed a case of white corn syrup every three months, and another a ten-gallon keg of whiskey twice a year.

Darsey issued tokens, sometimes called "Darsey gold," made of brass and redeemable for merchandise. The tokens were traded for beeswax, coonskins, cowhides, cotton, and corn and were spent in the store for food and other needs. He shipped in some goods by rail from Palestine and Nacogdoches. The store carried coffins, kept in a little frame shed called "the coffin house" nearby.

City ordinances at the turn of the century dictated part of the street scenes in front of the store. They specified that "all residents must remove their livestock from the streets; all males between 21 and 45 in the city are subject to street work for five days or $5.00; and the speed of the train must not exceed ten miles per hour in the city limits."

The train brought in traveling drummers, and the city required "from every traveling person selling patent or other medicines $1.50 per day or $6.25 for each three months." The train may also have brought to Grapeland Johnny Clifton of Bertram, better known as Buster Brown. With his little dog Tige, the two traveled all over the country to promote Buster Brown Shoes, often posing in front of each town's general store for a photograph as they did in Grapeland.

The bank robbery of 1910 shocked the town when thieves made off with around $10,000, but no other event hurt more of the town's residents than did the 1913 fire. Starting in the Palace of Sweets, a candy store-cafe on Front Street, the nighttime fire destroyed fifteen businesses and the Goodson Hotel. People flocked to the scene to try to save their property, but by daybreak the major business section of town lay in ashes.

Rebuilding began immediately. Darsey moved his plow points, buggy whip rack, tobacco cutter, and other salvaged merchandise into two box cars while he built the new store, a sturdy brick structure measuring 86 feet by 125 feet. He made the walls three-bricks thick, with corbeled brick detailing across the front. Towering iron columns supported the high, pressed tin ceiling, painted silver.

He used oak flooring and built a wide platform across the back of the store for the office. One side of the store was designed to hold groceries, household items, and farming needs; the other side for dry goods and clothing. Display cases included a heavy, oval case for Merrick's thread and an elaborate white and mirrored display case to show the latest in ladies' gloves and jewelry.

Outside, white marble wainscoting supported large display windows, and black and white tiles outlined the recessed entrance. A cast-iron doorplate marked the store's place in Grapeland history: "George E. Darsey — 1913."

By 1917, a Grapeland newspaper item reflected the town's moral and social values:

> Grapeland has a bicycle brigade, consisting of about fifteen boys from eight to fifteen years of age. The clayed streets are not good enough for them, so they up and come tearing down the sidewalk in front of the stores like a bunch of Apache Indians, demanding the right of way, and even ladies have to get out of the way of these riders, many times being forced to get off the sidewalk. On Saturday, it is a common thing to see a big yearling boy run against a lady with his wheel. The parents of every boy who has a wheel know it is not right to allow this practice and should prohibit it.

Merchants along Front Street were proud of the row of new sycamores in front of their businesses, and another newspaper editorial reminded parents and children of their duties as Grapeland citizens:

> The sycamore shade trees along Main Street were set out by our citizens to beautify the town and furnish shade during the hot summer months. They are yet young and should receive the greatest care and attention, and it should be the duty of everyone, children and all, to jealously guard their growth. However, we are sorry to say that Tuesday night some mischievous boys stripped one of these beautiful shade trees of its foliage, and today it stands out as an ugly monument to their deviltry. Boys, don't ever be guilty of such an ungentlemanly act again. Parents, do you know it was not your boy? Do you know where your boy is after the shades of night have fallen? Boys who make a habit of lying around town at night with associates of questionable character will sooner or later come to grief.

Grapeland was incorporated in 1924, the same year that Texas Power and Light Company started the high line for Crockett to Grapeland. The new mayor in his oath of office swore that he had "not fought a duel with deadly weapons within this state nor without it." In the newspaper, citizens were asked, "What will ye do with Grapeland? Are you ready to enter into that great spirit of brotherly love and cooperation in serving the town and its surrounding territory?"

Even during the difficult years of the 1930s, George Darsey, Jr., by then operating the store, continued to let customers charge on their accounts. Today, George's son Charley uses the same little wooden drawers under the old National cash register to file his customers' charges, although in the store's office, now removed from its platform perch to a front corner, a computer holds the store's records.

The past surrounds today's shoppers at Darsey's. The tin ceiling, tall iron columns, and the original floor are as impressive as ever. The office platform is now partitioned from the rest of the store to provide storage space, and the adjoining room that once carried high-button shoes and piece goods is used only for storage.

Modern merchandise includes all kinds of evidences of progress: refrigerators, television sets, film, electrical appliances, paperbacks, and packaged groceries. On one shelf, locally produced ribbon cane syrup in cans reminds us of what early-day shoppers found when they came to Darsey's, but a recent full-page ad in the *Grapeland Messenger* describes grocery items they would not recognize.

When Grapeland was incorporated in 1924, the newspaper challenged its citizens to invest their energies and money in the town's future. "As neighbors and friends, anxious to achieve something that will be worthwhile to those who are to live after us, we should now be ready to start reinforcing the foundation of a good town . . . What will ye do with Grapeland?"

How about the same family running a general store filled with all the townspeople's necessities for over 100 years?

# 14 | Hye General Store and Post Office

*. . . when the Secret Service were around, I'd call him "Mr. President."*

— Levi Deike

HYE   It is not unusual for a general store to be combined with a post office in small towns, but probably none anywhere has received as much attention as the one at Hye between Johnson City and Fredericksburg.

The first general store at Hye was founded by Hiram "Hye" Brown in 1880. The post office was established in 1866. In 1904, Brown built the present store that often causes motorists to slow down and stop when they see the little white building with its painted red and green Bavarian metal work. If they climb the three steps onto the front porch and read the historical medallions by the door, they discover that this is the post office where a future president mailed his first letter at the age of four. Born close to nearby Stonewall, Lyndon Johnson probably visited the store often with his mother. Later, he would return to visit, even selecting the front porch as the site to swear-in Postmaster General Lawrence O'Brien in 1965. It is rare that a postmaster general is sworn-in outside of Washington.

Levi Deike has been postmaster in Hye for over fifty years. He and brother Frederick acquired the store and post office from their father, Fritz, who bought it from Hiram Brown in 1923. Levi remembers LBJ long before his Washington days.

"He played on the ball team with me and my

*Between Johnson City and Fredericksburg, the Hye store and post office make travelers slow down and stop to admire its red and green Bavarian metal work. If they read the historical marker by the door, they discover this is where a future president mailed his first letter.*

eight brothers," he says. "He never got tired."

Even so, the future president could not make the trip in 1936, when the Deike brothers went as far as the quarter finals of the National Brothers Baseball Tournament in Wichita, Kansas. Besides, Levi adds, he wasn't eligible.

Asked if he and the president remained friends in their adult lives, Deike says, "Yes, when he'd come by to visit, I would always call him Lyndon

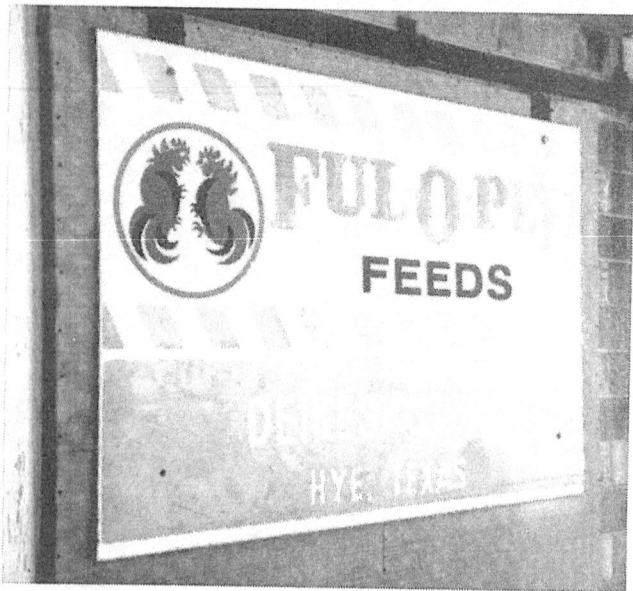

*Postmaster Levi Deike still sells a lot of feed, hardware, and harnesses.*

brothers baseball team.

Under the ornate, tin ceiling, painted silver, hang dusty reminders of life around Hye in earlier days: a buggy whip holder, horse shoes, harnesses, a Coats' thread case filled with drawers of spool cotton. Levi still uses the huge bolt rack with its many little drawers. In the back he has the original Michigan cash register and a Blue Mule tobacco cutter.

Today, the store carries a few groceries, blue jeans, and cowboy hats, but mostly its longest-selling item: feed of various kinds. At the back of the store, a sign lists what is available and is a good description of the region's main pursuits: corn, sow blox, calf nip, salt, deer blocks, pig starter, and turkey feed.

The Deike store is a quiet, relaxing place. Customers wander in and out, help themselves to corn and other feed, filling big sacks out on the porch by scale and the FULL-O-PEP sign. Levi and his wife won eight nice trips from the Quaker Oats people, he says, for selling feed. Above his desk hang awards for leadership from Wayne Feeds. "Won a bunch of those," he says matter-of-factly.

Hye and its surrounding farms once produced a lot of cotton. The rusting cotton gin across the street sits next to the old dance hall. A 100-year-old tree grows through the tin roof of the side building where the Deikes sold beer and soda pop to the crowds of Saturday night dancers. Levi remembers one Fourth of July dance in the 1920s when 380 couples came from all around to dance to the brass oompah band. In those days, brother Edwin ran the service station next door to the dance hall. Now, faded letters on the front of the corrugated tin dance hall are barely legible: "NEXT DANCE — SATURDAY."

Alongside the Hye store and post office, behind the big yellow house where Frederick lives in his parents' home, a narrow road winds south through the hills to Blanco. Levi recalls when cattle from the area were driven down that road "all the way to San Antonio."

As cars whoosh by on busy U.S. Highway 290, it is hard to imagine herds of cattle and oompah bands and a little boy who would grow up to be president, mailing a letter in the post office at the back of the Hye store. But Levi and Frederick regularly paint the red and green Bavarian design that the craftsman Schupp made, just so people will stop and be reminded that this little building beside the highway is no ordinary place.

when we were talking in private, but when the Secret Service were around, I'd call him 'Mr. President.' "

Faded photographs and newspaper clippings in the store remember the event. The *New York Herald Tribune* featured it on the front page November 4, 1965, with a photo of LBJ, O'Brien, Deike, and other officials on the front porch. A framed map titled "LBJ Country" hangs near a photo of the Deike

*An old buggy whip rack underneath the painted, pressed tin ceiling holds only dusty horseshoes today.*

# T. C. Lindsey & Company Store

*The Disney people wanted to buy everything we have, but nothing is for sale.*

— Sam Vaughan

JONESVILLE   Out on the long front porch, tacked to the bulletin board, a small notice offers a fifty-dollar reward for the recovery of a blue-tick hound named "Old Blue." (Look for the notch in his left ear.) As I step inside the T. C. Lindsey & Company Store, I think I'll ask them about Old Blue, see if he has been found, but then I'm too busy taking it all in. Like a lot of other visitors, I say something like "Good Glory!" It is like walking into one of those "see how many different things you can find" pictures. My eyes sweep around the room — big as an airplane hangar — over the counters piled with a melange of gimme caps, T-shirts, jeans, old-fashioned sun bonnets, and groceries. Lining the high top shelves and covering the top wall of the room, ancient farm tools and household items — churns, crocks, barrels, old patent medicine bottles. I quickly forget Old Blue.

This granddaddy of all old general stores in the state is located in the remnants of Jonesville, southeast of Marshall, about five miles north of Waskom. It is just off Interstate 20 on Farm Road 134 at a gentle curve in the road, only a deep breath away from the Louisiana border. In 1937 a record 2,976 bales were ginned at the big gin still standing across the road from the store. In those days, the store was a homestyle bank and loan agency for farmers, the main office and weigh station for the cotton gin, a polling place, meeting hall, and a general gathering place to talk about cotton prices, government interference, and the latest town news. But government control finally did Jonesville in, and in 1973 the gin processed four bales of cotton and closed down permanently.

Sam and Tom Vaughan are the store owners, and their roots go way back with the store. Before the Texas and Pacific Railroad came through from Marshall to Jonesville on its route to Shreveport, there was a cabin store up the road owned by partners Jones and Estes. In 1870 Sam and Tom's grandfather, Dr. Samuel Floyd Vaughan, purchased a half interest in the store, and around the turn of the century, their uncle, T. C. Lindsey, took over. Sam hired on in 1928 as a $50-a-month bookkeeper, then became a co-owner ten years later. Tom dropped out

*Stepping into the T. C. Lindsey & Company Store in Jonesville is like walking into one of those "see how many different things you can find" pictures.*

of the oil business in 1947 to become the third partner. When Lindsey died in 1948, the brothers divided the ownership and have been keeping the store filled with new merchandise and antiques ever since.

The disappearance of cotton farming apparently hasn't affected the store one bit — especially since the "movie people," as Sam calls them, discovered Jonesville. In 1970 Walt Disney Productions filmed *Bayou Boy* inside the store, and in 1979, *The Pond.* Another film company took advantage of the barn-

*"Mr. Sam" and Tom Vaughan enjoy telling visitors about the antique merchandise, but "nothing is for sale."*

size building with its enormous supply of antiques available for props and filmed *Stroke of Murder* there in 1974. Not only was this a perfect spot for filming in a near-ghost town with old buildings readily adaptable for repainting and remodeling according to the film makers' needs, but Sam, Tom, and the nice ladies who work in the store were agreeable to taking bit parts. Sam played the storekeeper in *The Pond* and again in *The Evictors,* shot in 1979. Sybil, one of the clerks, had a small part in the television movie "Long Hot Summer," filmed in 1985.

Before I go into one of the side rooms, I notice a sign: "Collectables Not for Sale." When Sam leads the way and I step in, I know how archaeologist Howard Carter must have felt when he first peered into King Tut's tomb. "Wonderful things!" he said when he saw the jumble of Egyptian treasures. In the store's side room, piled in dusty heaps and leaning against each other, are also "wonderful things." Sam holds up a child's 1921 tricycle. "Disney wanted to buy this," he says casually. Old farm tools with worn handles lean like thick jackstraws against what must have once been a beautiful wicker baby carriage. Sam pats it tenderly. "I raised three daughters from that buggy."

Tom joins us. Among the hodgepodge, I identify a tiny child's chair, now a faded red, covered with dust; old license plates; a hand-operated cotton gin; two old side saddles; a wicker doll buggy; a shoeshine bench; a split-dash churn. "Mama's," Tom says. "I used to work it. Always liked to hear it go 'ka-thump!' That was when the butter came."

I ask what they still sell that was sold in the early days of the store. Tom tells me, "Oh lots of things: woodstoves, washboards — two sizes — harnesses, whips, 'thunder jugs' — they call 'em 'combinettes' today." (I know what he means, but my grandmother had still another name for the jar that went under the bed.)

Sam picks up a piece of heavy, rusted metal. I can't identify it. "During the Civil War," he explains, "there was a rail line from Jonesville up to Caddo Lake, north of here. But they took up the rails between here and there to make armaments." The piece of metal takes on new meaning.

They lead me back into the big room. More merchandise, new and old. Anything that people have worn, used, or needed since the turn of the century, Sam and Tom have at least one. They don't carry things like stereos or cars, airplane tickets or health foods, but that is about all they don't have.

Sam wants to show me "Mr. Sam's play pretties," things which are strictly his and "don't belong to the store." He is the collector here, Tom has already told me. In glass cases and in another side room, Sam shows me, among other things, a ballot box from the store's days as a polling place, a burial suit from an Oklahoma City funeral home, his aunt's high-top shoes, a railroad caboose key, bitters bottles, an Edison light bulb, a Civil War cavalry sword he bought from "an old Negro lady" (my imagination soars, wondering where she got it), lead, iron and brass knuckles, four- and eight-gauge shotgun shells. "The Disney people wanted to buy everything we have," Sam says, "but nothing is for sale." They must have wept.

Out in the big room, I look around to see what *is* for sale. Underneath the shelf of patent medicine bottles, most of them long empty, is canned soup, coffee, dishwashing detergent, polish remover, chewing tobacco, post cards, and sunglasses. On counters, packages of sweet rolls, potato chips, Thermos jugs, electrical appliances — things the users of the farm tools on the wall could not have imagined. Near the top of a shelf is a reminder of how far back some of the products go: a Morton's salt box from the days when the little girl first started carrying her umbrella.

Sam shows me a 1913 license plate, and in his slow, soft East Texese, describes the state license plate department man who offered him a fancy price for it. "Called back to see if I'd change my mind if he raised the price. I wouldn't."

Upstairs, a balconied, partial floor holds clothing for sale as it has been for all the years since the store was built around 1922: work clothes and shoes, khaki pants, jeans, overalls, anything an outdoor working man could want.

When "Long Hot Summer" was being filmed in Jonesville, the "movie people" almost wore out their welcome. In a small nook of the store is the Jonesville post office. One day during the filming, Postmaster Reba Nolan heard the pulley squeaking on the flagpole outside. She stuck her head out to see what was going on, only to find a member of the film crew unceremoniously lowering the flag. She asked him what he was doing, and he explained that he was taking it down because it was fluttering in the wind and making a noise that was interfering with the day's shooting.

"I told him he could shinny up the pole and hold it still if he wanted to, but he darned sure wasn't taking it down."

The man raised the flag back up, but in a little while, another crew member came over to the post office and offered to "compensate" Reba is she would let them take it down.

"I told them that would be bribing a federal official," Reba says. That was the end of that, and Reba became Jonesville's "Barbara Fritchie," the heroine of the poem who was equally defiant of anyone fooling around with the American flag. News stories of the incident brought a flood of mail to the little post office, commending Reba's defense of the flag.

You can spend a day in the Lindsey store and not see everything. Or hear all of Mr. Sam's stories. One thing is for sure: the T. C. Lindsey & Company Store has almost everything you would ever find in a shopping mall — and all under one roof. What they don't have, you probably don't need anyway. You leave wishing you could have been the first to discover the big, white clapboard store and the Vaughan brothers. But the "movie people," other writers, and who knows how many tourists beat you there. I hope they found Old Blue.

## 16 Lajitas Trading Post

*At the Lajitas Trading Post on the Mexican border, the most frequent greeting tourists hear is "Buenos días."*

*You can ponder the bullet holes in the walls, more likely from local celebrations and disagreements than from Mexican banditos.*

LAJITAS  "The man you need to talk to is out back skinning a javelina. You can go out and talk with him if you like."

This kind of friendliness and casual attitude toward the rugged, still-untamed Big Bend country of Texas pretty much sums up the Lajitas Trading Post in the little border village of Lajitas. But wild hogs, bobcats, panthers, and rattlesnakes, as well as two-legged predators, for years made the Texas-Mexico border along the Rio Grande a region that spawned both true adventure and tall tales.

Named by the Mexicans, the word *lajitas* means "little flagstones" (after the rock formations in the region). Before the two settlements with this name existed on opposite sides of the river, Comanche Indians were using the crossings, taking advantage of the river's smooth rock bottom.

Unique environments produce unique establishments. Early in the century, along this riverbank, a chain of remote stores sprang up from the southernmost tip of the state northwest along its border for several hundred miles. These stores drew

*On chilly days, visitors can sit around the old stove from Fort Russell up in Marfa — "Space heater — U.S. Army No. 1." It takes a while to see everything on the hole-pocked walls.*

customers from both sides of the river. Mexicans walked or rode donkeys from distant villages over roads that were little more than trails to obtain food and other necessities. While receipts ran into thousands of dollars annually, almost no money changed hands since most transactions were in barter. The Mexican customers lived off the land, and its products were their only wealth. They would load the backs of their burros with chino grass, wood, vegetables — anything they had to trade for essentials at the border stores.

In 1902 the *Alpine Avalanche* reported that "Lajitas is becoming quite a town. It has one store, a beer saloon, a schoolhouse with fifty pupils, and a custom house for the sub-district port of entry. Lajitas is the best river crossing between Del Rio and El Paso . . ." H. W. McGuirk, who was in the mining business in nearby Terlingua, built the Lajitas church at his own expense in 1901. He probably was also the builder of the store in 1902 and ran it for fifteen years.

Like the church, the store was built of adobe bricks with walls two feet thick. The flat, dirt roof was typical of adobe structures in the Southwest. In 1917 McGuirk sold the store to Thomas V. Skaggs, who may have been the one to add protective lime and sand plaster to the inside and outside walls. A 1917 photograph shows the neat little store, with its roof-supporting *vigas* extending outside the white stuccoed side, and the pile of lime still visible. Two large signs advertising Star Tobacco appear over the front door and on one side. The living quarters adjoining the store building show uncovered adobe with *vigas* across the front. Mounted on horseback are three Texas Rangers who had been in the Big Bend, investigating the Brite ranch raid by Mexican bandits.

During those early years, the floor inside was mostly dirt, and merchandise was stacked on boxes. Supplies came by long mule and wagon trains from Alpine on the Southern Pacific Railroad route to the north. It was a three-day trip, winding the 100 treacherous miles over mountainous terrain, only occasionally broken by flat plains.

The supply trains also brought goods to the cavalry post established at Lajitas in 1915 to guard the border and the western approach to the Terlingua quicksilver mines. Pancho Villa, the Mexican Robin Hood, had kept both sides of the border terrorized as leader of the Mexican revolution that began in 1910. Texas Rangers joined federal troops in trying to outwit Mexican and Anglo opportunists as they stole, swapped, and sold cattle, ammunition, and guns on both sides of the river.

While there is no proof that either Villa nor any of his men ever actually visited the Lajitas store, other bandits, smugglers, and common thieves were frequent transients and warranted the watchful eyes of Rangers, soldiers, customs guards, and border patrolmen.

During the years Tom Skaggs owned the store, he became postmaster and earned the respect of the little village. He furnished school supplies without charge to Lajitas children attending the one-teacher school on the bluff behind the store and encouraged the brightest ones to develop their talents. He also operated a candelilla wax factory from the candelilla plants across the river. Skaggs bequeathed the store

to Everett E. Townsend, a prominent Big Bend rancher, legislator, and peace officer. In 1949 Rex Ivey bought the store from the Townsends.

Ivey is a Big Bend rancher whose free barbecues and dances during the 1950s were attended by hundreds of guests from both sides of the river — so many, he says, that he finally had to discontinue them. Ivey added amenities to the store, such as a concrete floor inside and a concrete porch with a roof outside. From old stores that were closing, he purchased the cabinets that hold today's merchandise. He continued the candelilla wax business and in 1969 gave the store to his son Bill, who runs it today.

While Ivey likes to promote his image of a bearish old rancher who doesn't trust writers or film makers, underneath the crusty facade lies a man who feeds hungry animals along the highway, wild and domestic, and keeps small javelinas for pets. (Although he didn't take too kindly to his employee who killed the one that got out and turned nasty as javelinas are prone to do.) And sure, he let Willie Nelson borrow some of his antiques for a movie, but he surely would not sell them to the singer.

Bill Ivey runs the store much as it has always been run, keeping charge accounts for certain customers in an old black metal McCaskey file, exchanging pesos for dollars if he has to, and sacking candy to sell by the pound to his Mexican customers on payday.

There is one fairly recent addition. Clay Henry is a goat with more than a passing fondness for beer. Bring a can to the rocks just inside the pen in front of the store, pop the ring opening, and before you can say "Cheers," Clay Henry — as well as his fellow drinking buddies — are clambering over the rocks, heads hanging through the rail, mouths open. While his pals stand begging, Clay Henry, knowing he is the star of this show, holds the can or bottle between his teeth and chugalugs it in a matter of seconds. He knows his limit, though, and sometimes goes off in a shady corner of the pen to take a nap. In an unofficial mayoral race in Lajitas one year, Clay Henry won more votes than the single candidate.

The Lajitas Trading Post is another of those places where you need to stick around for a while to take in everything. While billiard balls plunk on the pool table on the porch, and pickups crunch to a stop on the gravel outside, it is fun to sit on the old wood-slatted chair and watch. Employees go in and out of the battered gate, barely hanging on with leather strip hinges, at the end of the counter. Customers wander in and out, none in a hurry. The smell of expensive perfume mixes with the odors of sweat and beer. A plump woman from Houston in designer jeans wants a souvenir. Mexican workers from the Lajitas tourist version of an Old West town visit with each other and store employees, the most frequent greeting *"Buenos días."* Wind-whipped motorcyclists ask for four cups of ice. An attractive, college-educated young artist says she is living in an adobe ruin in Terlingua so she can keep her horses and paint.

Tourists include suntanned river rafters, paying up on their raft rentals. Most customers want a cold drink or a snack, but they can also buy local cactus jelly, New Mexico pottery, Southwestern-style jewelry, and, of course, a T-shirt with the store logo on it. If it is a chilly day, they can sit around the old stove from Fort Russell up in Marfa — "Space Heater — U.S. Army No. 1." Some may need to buy film, diapers, fishing tackle, or canned goods.

The inside walls are pocked with holes, some from nails driven in to hold various things, near the stove a rusted-out, bottomless skillet. Beer signs decorate the walls throughout the store, some new, some old enough to attract the attention of collectors, many in Spanish: "Cerveza Coors."

From the ceiling hangs a miscellany of the past, some things of a type still in use: hangarias (the wood and cowhide strip baskets used to carry loads on donkeys' backs), a couple of ancient wooden saddles, dusty strings of dried red chile peppers, horse collars. Tucked into the rafters here and there are nests of barn swallows, which leave in September and return in March. While in Lajitas, they fly in and out of the little half-moon opening in the broken glass of the front door.

You know there must be a story behind many of the objects lying around the store. Who would have abandoned a dust-shrouded bass fiddle? How about the old saxophone and guitar hanging high on the wall? How did the three-foot-long rattlesnake meet its end before it was dried and mounted on the wall above the jukebox? Heavy, Mexican spurs hang over the front door between red chile pepper Christmas lights that stay up year round, an interesting juxtaposition of symbols. The door itself is battered and dirty and the threshold worn to a smooth, gray sheen from almost a century of use.

Except for times when someone is celebrating something, life around the Lajitas Trading Post is about as slow-paced as you will find anywhere. You can sit on the porch on the splintery church pew from Terlingua and watch the hanging catfish heads dry in the mesquite tree. Or you might read the warnings written in Spanish on the porch benches: "Please don't spit on the floor," "No drunks after 9:00." If it is summer, you may not want to read the temperature on the big thermometer by the door, the one that also tells you Dr. Barker's Horse Liniment is "good for mules and jackasses," too. You can ponder the bullet holes in the walls, more likely from local celebrations and disagreements than from Mexican banditos. Everyone is friendly — the store doesn't even keep guns in stock — and no revolution seems imminent. Pancho Villa would be plain bored.

# 17 Luckenbach Store

Let's go back to Luckenbach, Texas . . . where ain't nobody feelin' no pain.

LUCKENBACH  If Willie Nelson and Waylon Jennings hadn't put the song "Let's Go Back to Luckenbach, Texas" on the charts, the folks hadn't learned there really is such a place, the Highway Department might have had more success with their road signs. They gave up a long time ago trying to mark the turnoff onto FM 1376, south from U.S. Highway 290 west of Fredericksburg, to show travelers where Luckenbach is. People kept stealing the signs.

The late humorist-folk hero Hondo Crouch held the little crossroads in the public eye with chili cook-offs, festivals, and country-western dances in the old dance hall by the store. As Hondo said, "If you find Luckenbach, you have to be looking for it," but a lot of people look, and a lot of people find it.

Back when Luckenbach got started, of course,

the name did not evoke smiles. In 1849 Minna Engel opened a general store in the location to trade goods with the Indians. Meanwhile, a group of German immigrants from the Wester Forest in Germany left their town of Luckenbach, adopting the town's name for themselves. Moving out from Fredericksburg, the Luckenbachs came to this area where Jakob Luckenbach bought 593 acres of land on South Grape Creek. Minna's brother August and her fiance Carl Albert Luckenbach built the present store, and in 1858, another brother, Wilhelm, became postmaster. The post office was closed between 1869 and 1886, and when it reopened, the name of the settlement was changed from Grape Creek to Luckenbach.

The Luckenbachs were solid citizens. When Wilhelm became justice of the peace in 1865, his oath included the statement that he had "not fought a duel with a deadly weapon within this state nor out of it nor have I accepted a challenge to fight a

As early as 1849, a general store in Luckenbach was operated by Minna Engel to trade goods with Indians. By 1850
a post office was established by the Luckenbachs, newly arrived from Germany.

duel with deadly weapons."

Near the store, you can see further evidence of
the little community's busier days. On FM 1376 sits
the limestone school building where Jakob Luckenbach was a trustee. Across the rickety bridge over
Grape Creek by the store, you see the rusting cotton

In the Luckenbach store, visitors see the kinds of merchandise that shoppers found on sale when it was advertised as
a "First Class Country Store."

The Luckenbach store didn't sell coffins, but Hondo Crouch
added this one for its effect.

gin built in 1881, and closer to the store, the old
blacksmith shop and the outhouse.

An ad in the German-language newspaper in
Fredericksburg in 1902 described the store as a
"First Class Country Store." Walk along the narrow
aisle today and you can still see some of the kinds of
merchandise the store carried — dust-covered Texana, hanging from rafters, sitting on shelves and the
floor, leaning against the old walls. Watch a visitor
enter the shadowy interior for the first time, and
you see expressions varying from curiosity to disbelief. Squinting into the semidarkness, he may
glimpse at an old coffin resting on the rafters. (The
store did not carry them; Hondo brought this one in.)
On the shelves, old boxes of Rinso and Biz, a bottle of
Golden Relief ("for diahrrea and cuts and bruises —
68% alcohol, 22 minims of ether, 5 minims of chlo-
roform"), a lace-up corset, horse collars, horseshoes,
nails, high-topped women's shoes, a framed photograph of Nixon. None of these things for sale, of
course.

The old post office faces the aisle near the front
door, and at the nearby counter you can buy souven-
ier T-shirts and a picture of Hondo, Willie Nelson, or
the Alamo.

Step carefully, newcomer, as you pass through
the store. A man recently put his foot through a part

32

of the old floor. Slowly travel back to the bar section, through the door and under the longhorns and the sign reading "Everybody's Somebody in Luckenbach," and down the two steps into a kind of tilted nostalgia. It will take you a while to absorb it all.

On the walls are photos of Hondo and country-western celebrities. And there are posters, signs, and bumper stickers that read: "Say something good about America," "How can anyone so bad be so good at it?" "If you need credit, you don't need a beer, you need a job," "Texan for Secession," "Yield — it's more fun," and one in Spanish, *"La proxima vez su esposa"* ("Next time, bring your wife").

You also see gimme caps, some hanging on the head of a mounted African wildebeest, dried snake skins, license plates from all over, a stuffed armadillo, old and new beer signs. Behind the bar is a photograph of Crouch's daughter Becky Patterson and current Luckenbach owners, Kathy Morgan and Chris Graham, along with their spouses, bar manager Marge Mueller and her husband, and George, the young store employee — all of them posing on the store's front porch for a Justin boot ad.

In the center of the room sits the old Volcano stove around which locals such as Armin Engel, a descendant of the original owners, play daily dominoes. Armin recalls when they skated on Grape Creek in the early part of the century and when the post office had fifty to sixty regular boxes.

Marge Mueller is related to Engel, and recently they have had the chance to meet a lot of distant cousins. A few years ago, the Luckenbachs and Engels began having family reunions in Luckenbach, and when they all gather in the old Tanze Hall across the way for introductions and a covered dish lunch, the population of Luckenbach swells from the "city limit" sign number of "three" to over two hundred.

In 1986 the family dedicated a marker, erected in front of the store near the bronze bust of Hondo Crouch. The marker describes the founders and first settlers of Luckenbach and also pays tribute to Crouch for making the place famous "and promoting its rustic atmosphere."

There is a lot of that kind of atmosphere around Luckenbach, all right. You can sit out under the huge old trees behind the store and listen to the insects in the meadow or maybe to a guitar player who also found FM 1376. It is hard to imagine the place ever being very busy unless you happen to drop in for the Luckenbach family reunion or for the Ladies State Championship Chili Cookoff or the Valentine's Day Hug-In. As Willie and Waylon sing, it is a place where you can "get back to the basics of life" and where "ain't nobody feelin' no pain."

# 18 | Territorial Mercantile

*Maydelle and Dialville were about nippety-tuck.*
— Cullen Sherman

MAYDELLE   You have to be careful when you set out to find a town where the buildings are genuinely old — old as in fifty years or more. Things are not always what they seem, especially if "the movie people" have been there.

"The movie people," as the locals call them, are the film makers from California and Texas who like to use small towns for filming locations. Often they take buildings that are old to begin with and try to make them look even older. In Maydelle, for example, a private residence that was originally the town's 1911 bank was altered to look like an old hotel for a James Garner television movie. Before that film, the general store that was already of early-century vintage had been embellished to look even older, with rough, cedar posts and deer antlers across its false front and a misspelled "Territorial Merchantile" sign. Lest you have any doubt that this is a *real* country store, another sign proclaims

*The "movie people" occasionally alter storefronts to look even older and more rustic than they are. The East Texas store in Maydelle is a good example.*

"Territorial Mercantile" (spelled correctly here) over a red-white-and-blue Lone Star Feed-Fertilizer sign atop the corrugated gray tin roof. A Mobil Oil flying red horse completes the picture.

The wooden crossbar hitching post in front of the gasoline pumps outside the store seems a little contradictory, but the overall effect is what owner Jerry Graham wants. His adjoining cafe is also rustic and filled with photographs of movie stars and memorabilia from Maydelle's authentically old days.

The town dates back to the 1840s, if you count the four settlements that were eventually consolidated to form Maydelle. Pinetown, Java, Mt. Comfort, and Ghent all faded away for various reasons, and Maydelle was born in 1910, christened with the slightly altered name of Texas Governor Thomas M. Campbell's daughter.

In the late 1800s and early 1900s, the state of Texas built the railroad between the towns of Rusk and Palestine. Maydelle is located in between the two towns, and — like its neighbor Dialville a few miles north — it became a shipping point for tomatoes, with packing sheds near the railroad tracks. A former general store owner and Maydelle postmaster, J. Cullen Sherman remembers when the town also had a cotton gin and a lumber mill, a "peckerwood mill" as he calls it, run at first by steam, then gasoline.

The town at one time had thirty-seven stores of various kinds, a hotel, and a bank. Did the townspeople of Maydelle and Dialville get along? Were the towns competitive? "Oh, they sometimes got crossways, naturally," Sherman says.

What about size? Did one town try to grow faster than the other, be more progressive?

"I'd say they were about nippety-tuck," he observes.

Sherman remembers when his store sold wagons, stoves, tools, clothing, and caskets. He let Maydelle people buy feed and fertilizer and "pay when their crops came in" just as his father who ran the store before him had done. "Back then," he says, "the government didn't help anybody. I sometimes wonder how they made it."

Maydelle's present-day business section faces U.S. Highway 84, which runs through town alongside the railroad tracks. Of the several early general stores, Sherman's former business is now a crafts shop, and only two remain open as stores, including the Territorial Mercantile.

A sign over the screen doors says "Clean Beds — 25¢," but that is just to remind you that this is a *really old place*. Inside you don't have to be convinced. Big, glass candy jars line one counter, and some of the jars contain penny candy; that is, candies that cost only a *penny* apiece, things like jawbreakers, licorice whips, and chewing gum with your fortune inside the wrapper. Salt and popcorn are sold in bulk, and local tomatoes and cantaloupes are on sale during the summer months, potatoes year round. You can also buy minnows, worms, hardware, tools, and almost any necessary drug or grocery item you want.

If you are a first-time shopper, you may find your concentration diverted by some of the items mixed in with the regular merchandise. Yes, that is a stuffed rooster on top of one shelf, next to the scales basket that can't weigh anything because it is hanging from a hook in the ceiling. Lots of things must have a story behind each one if there were time to find out: two pine cones hang from the ceiling with strings. Next to the fat, brown stove, a stack of huge innertubes for renting to take to the nearby lake.

Some honestly old signs hang behind modern canned goods, one advertising Bull Durham Smoking Tobacco, caricaturing blacks in a way no longer acceptable, but you can still buy Bull Durham.

Several people in Maydelle ask if you have heard the black panther scream since you came to town. Fortunately no, but he's out there, they say. "Several folks have heard him, may be more than one, probably is. Our postmaster even saw one a man had killed. Stretched the length of a pickup truckbed."

Some scenes from the television series "Dallas" were filmed in Maydelle in recent years, using the store, the depot across the road, and the Texas State Railroad. The railroad still operates with a steam engine and passenger cars to take travelers on a scenic journey between Palestine and Rusk. Sometimes it stops briefly in Maydelle for a "shootout" and a "train robbery."

Waving at the passengers as the engine puffs through town is one of the things you can do in Maydelle. Or mail a post card in the blue, playhouse-size post office, which is also on the main road. The cafe has a player piano and good homestyle food. Unless "the movie people" are there, things are pretty quiet, and no one seems to care much any more whether Maydelle and Dialville are "nippety-tuck" or not.

# Seigmund's General Store

Seigmund's General Store in McDade was once the Mc-Dade depot during the years when the town was the shipping point for freight and cotton to and from Smithville and Bastrop.

*The trains built the country, but the highways ruined the little towns.*

— Tom Dungan

Tom Dungan ran the store for many years, and he moved the depot across the road when the original store burned. He remembers when the passenger trains stopped in Mc-Dade four times a day.

McDADE  Before railroads, beginning with the first track laid in 1852, moving goods overland to the general mercantile stores was slow and often next to impossible. Gigantic wagons overturned, trying to stay in ruts of the well-worn trails across prairies and through forests. Mules and oxen sometimes stumbled and fell into quagmires, spilling wooden barrels and crates and damaging merchandise. When freight did arrive, the rates could be as high as one cent per mile per hundred pounds. Then the railroad began sending arteries into the state from the southeast near present-day Houston, bringing lifeblood to little towns like McDade.

By the time the Texas and New Orleans Railroad reached McDade in 1871, Austin, thirty-five miles to the west, had almost 5,000 people, and another railroad line stretched on to San Antonio, which had a population of 12,000. During the first part of the 1870s, more than 100,000 new settlers from the southern states came to Texas, and railroad mileage grew with the population.

McDade was first known as Tie City or Tie Town because it was the collection center for ties and logs cut for the expansion of the railroad. The town was laid out in 1871, incorporated in 1873, and renamed McDade after James McDade, the railroad lawyer. Between 1871 and 1886, the town became the shipping point for freight and cotton to and from Smithville and Bastrop.

To see any old town's earliest beginnings, searchers need only to find the railroad tracks in the center of the town's original business district. If the depot is still standing, that spot is the location of the town's first real heartbeat. In McDade it is possible to find, at the same time, both the depot and the oldest general store still in operation because they are one.

Seigmund's General Store was formerly T. E. Dungan's Grocery, run by Tom Dungan, who moved the depot across the road to the location of a store that had burned. Today's owners are George and Jona Lee Seigmund, but talk to Tom to learn how the town was when passenger trains came through and stopped four times a day.

At one time McDade had five mercantile stores, a bank, two blacksmith shops, two cotton gins, a school, livery stable, a pottery factory, and a factory for making charcoal furnaces. Across the railroad tracks in another row of buildings were a millinery shop, a hotel, confectionery store, and other mercantile stores. Along the side street by the Seigmund store, a funeral home used a horse-drawn hearse, Dungan remembers. Down the block, the 1870 Rock Front Saloon and stagecoach stop put McDade into all the guidebooks because of the 1883 lynching and shootout.

On Christmas Eve of that year, a group of area vigilantes captured and hanged three of the men who had been killing and causing general misery for a long time in the area. Christmas morning brought a shootout in the saloon between some of the killers' friends and law-abiding McDade citizens. As they passed through town that day, travelers on the train from Houston to Austin saw five bodies, stretched out on the depot loading platform.

Tom remembers the days when the depot had two segregated waiting rooms and separate entrances for blacks and whites. The store's present-day front counter was formerly the telegraph and ticket counter, and owner Jona Lee Seigmund uses the ticket drawer for odds and ends. A new ceiling was installed because the old one reached to the rafters of the building's roof.

Under the old ticket window, a worn bench that once sat out in front of another store now provides a comfortable place to sit, have a cup of the store's coffee, and meet a good many McDade citizens. A descendant of one of the lynching victims is a frequent customer, but she is not eager to discuss the episode. However, almost everyone that comes in had a part in a recent television movie filmed in McDade, and this is a subject everyone is willing to talk about. I ask Tom if he was in it.

"Yeah," he smiles, "I was a beer-drinkin', pipe-smokin' checker player. I don't do any of those things."

Someone wants to know why I didn't come to McDade's annual July watermelon festival. I missed the parade, barbecue, crowning of two queens, and the street dance. Maybe next year.

On the bulletin board outside the black screen door, townspeople can tack up funeral notices; other signs against the depot's peeling yellow paint tell about the wrestling matches in Smithville and Giddings, announce that Capitol Feeds are sold inside, give the number to call to have your septic tank pumped, tell where ducks are for sale, and inform citizens who is running for district attorney.

At the other end of the building, another sign lets people know that Railway Express once serviced the town, that Butter Krust bread was once sold here, and that watermelons still are. Tom says they used to ship a lot of watermelons by rail to other states from McDade.

Outside the store, Tom touches the side of the old yellow building tenderly. "I hope they don't paint her," he says. He looks across the road at the quiet railroad tracks and the vacant spaces beyond where stores once lined the other road facing the tracks. He does some more remembering. "People used to come down every time a passenger train stopped. Everyone wanted to know who was going someplace and who had been someplace."

Tom worked for the railroad before he became a merchant, so he is probably sadder than most people to see the gradual fading away of the railroad. Today, no trains at all rattle through McDade.

"The trains built the country," Tom says, "but the highways ruined the little towns."

He is right, of course. McDade's quiet Main Street, where Seigmund's General Store sells watermelons and hardware and Capitol Feeds, used to be the main road to Austin.

# 20 | J. B. McDonald General Merchandise

*. . . everything from the cradle to the grave.*

NECHES  Around 1838, a group of North Carolinians brought their wagons across the Neches River to near Brushy Creek and put down their first Texas roots. Among them was Murdoch McDonald, who soon married and started a family. In 1871 he moved his family a few miles south to Nechesville on the dirt road between Jacksonville and Palestine. That same year he jump-started the town by deeding 300 acres of his land to the International Railroad Company to extend its line and lay out a town. McDonald stipulated that the railroad build a depot and give him three town lots. In 1872 the railroad reached Nechesville, the town was platted, and a depot, post office, and McDonald's hotel were built.

The town's name was changed to Neches in 1892, and in 1897 one of McDonald's sons, John Bethune, built a fine red-brick mercantile store facing the railroad tracks and the main road. The bricks were made from river clay and fired in McDonald's own kiln. Soon after the store was furnished, the adjoining bank was built, using the same bricks. The store has been run continuously by McDonald sons

*In Neches, J. B. McDonald described his store as carrying "everything from the cradle to the grave."*

and a grandson. Today, it is operated by Bethune McDonald and his mother Mrs. Brice McDonald.

Until his death in 1986, Brice McDonald, John B.'s son, had the store for nearly sixty years. During this time, he collected and saved some of the store's earliest merchandise and furnishings. In 1986 a group of Neches residents, led by Sadie Phillips, assembled a store museum as a Texas Sesquicentennial project. It is located in the back half of the store and in the huge, log, feed storage building behind the store.

John B. McDonald's slogan for the store was his statement that he carried everything for townsfolk "from the cradle to the grave." The collection of store antiques in the McDonald Museum proves it.

Brice McDonald used to tell how his father would often be awakened in the middle of the night at his home near the store by someone wanting to buy a casket. (In the museum are the stands on which caskets were placed at funerals.) Sometimes the nighttime awakenings were from a couple wanting to be married, since John was justice of the peace for many years.

One of the oldest family treasures on display in the museum is the spinning wheel that was used by a McDonald family member. Rachel Richardson Freeman was born in Arkansas when the North Carolina wagon train was en route to Texas. She used the spinning wheel in Texas during the Civil War.

Some of the items on display have stories behind them. On a wall, two curious poles catch the visitor's eye and have to be explained. Yes, that really is a preserved bear claw and a puma claw. They were used by Brice McDonald's friend McMartin Albert to plant bear and puma tracks around the town, indisputable evidence that one of these fearsome creatures had come out of the piney woods and could make an appearance at any time. To alert citizens, area newspapers carried the story, and local men carried shotguns.

The Winchester rifle was a useful weapon in the days when wild animals were common sights around Neches. One may have been used to kill the snarling wild boar mounted on a wall near an old poster advertising the Winchester.

Another McDonald museum item with a story is the large, handmade, wooden bread bowl. When the McDonald wagon left North Carolina, there was no room for the essential family possession inside the wagon, so it was attached to the underside and survived the long, rough journey to Texas.

Storekeepers at the turn of the century often kept irregular hours in order to accommodate their customers. Cotton farmers would haul their cotton to Neches to sell it, then spend their money at the end of the day in McDonald's store.

"They often shopped at night by the light of coal oil lamps," Brice McDonald recalled. "They'd fill those big, wooden shipping boxes with overalls, shoes, piece goods, all kinds of things."

Shoppers could buy two different kinds of coal oil, white and red. McDonald used a red powder to color the coal oil and "got a nickel a gallon more for the red kind."

Over the years, other buildings that once faced the road on either side of the store have either burned or have been torn down, but next door the still solid bank is now used for Masonic Lodge meetings. Once, in the early 1900s, a bank robbery prompted Mrs. McDonald to grab all the store's money and hide it under the feed sacks in the log storage building. However, the robbers did not bother the McDonalds.

In the McDonald store, as in other general stores, were standard furnishings that are today as sturdy as in the years when they were used daily. In the museum: a wooden vinegar barrel and pump, used to fill customers' gallon jugs; wooden packing barrels and boxes; a tobacco cutter; an octagonal wooden hardware cabinet; scales; a counter display case for thread; an ornate, brass-and-iron cash register; a heavy counter rack for dispensing wrapping paper; and a massive butcher block.

The neighboring town of Palestine wanted Brice McDonald to lend them his antiques for one of the Dogwood Trails exhibits, but he declined and lived to cut the ribbon at the opening of his store museum. Some Neches residents still don't much like the fact that Palestine bought their depot to use as a tourist center in Reagan Park and removed the Neches name from it.

Outside the screen doors of J. B. McDonald & Son General Merchandise, Neches is much quieter these days than any time since its 1897 beginnings. No big wagons piled high with bales of cotton, waiting for the gin down the road. No one needing a casket nor wanting to be married by the justice of the peace. Hardly anyone sits on the worn, low bench to exchange news or watch the trains go by. Not as many shoppers come in as before. But in the museum and in the store, John Bethune McDonald's descendants gently display many things his family and other Neches people used and enjoyed "from the cradle to the grave."

# 21 | San Fernando House of Antiques and Treasures

*In 1906 Pontotoc in Central Texas had a newspaper, a movie theater, a post office, and a recently closed school, the San Fernando Academy. Its general store faced the main road just as it does today, but now it sells only "antiques and treasures."*

*Buried him right on the spot, right out there in the woods on the mountain. I can take you there right now if you want me to.*

— Sam Metzger

*Rarely are family antiques for sale in Texas's general stores but in the San Fernando House of Treasures and Antiques, this ancient rawhide strip chair is.*

PONTOTOC   It is surprising how many people say they have never heard of Pontotoc. If you are heading south toward Llano from Brady on State Highway 71, you can't miss it. Well, yes you can. If you are in a hurry or are wishing you had turned off earlier to check out Voca or Fredonia, you just might whoosh on by.

There used to be quite a little town here not long after M. R. Kidd from Pontotoc, Mississippi, named it. *Pontotoc* means "grapes on a vine," but it probably didn't matter to M. R. Kidd whether or not there were any grapes around. The earliest cemetery stones are dated 1859, and for some reason all the others read from 1890 on.

The San Fernando Academy with 200 students only lasted seven years, from 1883 to 1890. In 1906 there was a newspaper, *The Country News,* and Steve Ficklin ran a movie theater at the end of the little strip of empty buildings where today the post office and cafe are located. It was a growing town, but then, as you have already guessed, the railroad passed it by, and that was the end of hope for a prosperous future for Pontotoc.

The current *Texas Almanac* says Pontotoc has a population of 206, but the locals who should know say they have "fifty voters, total population seventy-

five, counting the kids." Nevertheless, most of these divide their time between the post office/cafe and the building that once housed a general store. The San Fernando House of Antiques and Treasures sounds a lot fancier than it is, and "fancy" is not the word for the charm and interest of Pontotoc.

Zella Metzger and Isabelle Polk own the store. Isabelle is usually behind the counter where you can buy soft drinks and snacks. Zella watches over the store and spends some of her time in one of the several worn easy chairs around the coffee table up front. So do several of the town's most loquacious citizens.

If you enjoy local stories, Sam Metzger is your man. I didn't have time to hear all the details, but he was eager to tell me about the man who froze to death in the nearby woods and "stayed out there forty-two days before we found 'im." It seems the man asked for shelter from the owners of a cabin in the woods during a really cold night, but they turned him away. (The cabin was small, see, and the man's wife was about to have a baby.) The traveler never made it to his destination, and when this was discovered, Sam joined others "in a posse," and eventually they found him.

"What did you do with him?" I wanted to know.

"Buried him right on the spot, right out there in the woods on the mountain. I can take you there right now if you want me to."

I said I didn't have time this trip, maybe next time. Then I asked about one of the major crops in the area — peanuts. I had noticed a bowl full of them on the big, round coffee table in front of us. Why didn't they sell them at the store? Sam had a story on that subject, too. "It's the government's fault. Those Communists up in Washington. They won't let us." He spoke with great conviction, so I didn't question him.

While I walked around the store and noted it was a collector's heaven, no matter what you collect, a singer on the store's radio crooned happily, "I'm gonna wake up in your arms tomorrow. Thank you for taking me to Paradise!"

From tables, from the old vegetable bin when the store sold groceries, I picked up one, then another of the random clutter of "antiques and treasures," half hoping I would find some priceless something at a bargain, but knowing I wouldn't. Zella Metzger may have the same relaxed easiness of other small-town people, but she knows her antiques. I had noticed two collectors' books on her coffee table in which the current worth and going price for everything from Fiestaware to first-edition Nancy Drew books is listed. I asked about an old straight chair with a seat made from rawhide strips. Zella's grandfather made it, and to me, that seemed a treasure without price, but it was for sale.

While I continued to look at old bottles, tarnished flatware, costume jewelry, and a World War I canteen, another longtime Pontotoc citizen offered to take me to see what he called the old "Pony Express" station on a small mountain nearby. I had to turn down that invitation, too. I wanted to go take another picture of the old San Fernando Academy ruins behind the store, just as I do every time I am in Pontotoc. Then there is Betty Waldon's cafe across the way — even an old tire to swing on if I were younger. You would be surprised how much there is to do in a town with only fifty voters.

## 22 | Poolville General Store

*It is too bad that dust layers can't be measured like circles in a tree trunk to determine their age and the age of what lies beneath.*

POOLVILLE If you pull up alongside the little town park and go through the squeaky, silver-painted turnstile, you get the feel of Poolville right away. In the center of the park you will find the memorial to Dr. W. J. Sparks, who owned the land the town was built on and had it platted and recorded in 1901. According to the words on the memorial, he was respected and appreciated by Poolville's citizens. Another marker lists Poolville people who pledged various amounts of money from five dollars to five hundred dollars for "the capture and delivery, dead or alive, to the American authorities — the German Kaiser." This marker is dated 1917.

At one end of the park, a large, pink-blossomed mimosa tree leans over the wall next to the windmill. Through it you can catch your first glimpse of the general store. If it weren't for the few pickups and cars coming and going and the big, modern ice dispenser and newspaper racks in front, you would think the store was closed and had long ago stopped

*If it weren't for a few pickups, the big ice dispenser, and the newspaper racks in front, you'd think the store in Poolville had long ago stopped arguing with time.*

arguing with time.

The store and what remains of the buildings on the same side of the square escaped both of the fires that destroyed businesses and homes in 1936 and again in the 1960s. A couple of doors down from the store, a crumbling old barber shop, its red and white

39

*At one time, a milliner had her shop on the balcony, and ladies lifted their skirts as they climbed the stairs to try on hats.*

paint faded and peeling, does not need the sign that reads "Closed." Around the corner, the white frame United Methodist Church is holding funeral services for a Poolville native who had moved to Fort Worth but was returned to her hometown for burial. The cemetery is near the church, along with an old brush arbor, no longer roofed with tree branches but with corrugated tin.

Poolville began as a large watering hole for cattle drives heading north and west. The spring-fed pool served as a wash tub for the earliest pioneer women in the 1850s. By the 1870s, the town was well established with a saloon, church, sawmill, school, and a store. By 1906, the town had a population of over 400, with names such as Wilkins, Seaberry, Deal, Taylor, Upton, Brittain, and Turpin.

Owner Mary Lou Wilkins thinks her store was built around 1883. The floor, more than anything, suggests the store's age. Worn places are patched with tin, the surface buckling and tilting, giving under your feet like a moving ship. The store may have been built by V. A. Seaberry, then run by a Mr. Freely and finally by Mary Lou's grandfather, "Pop" Carter, and her father, who called it Carter's Store.

Today, the store sells snack food, soft drinks, bread, and toiletries, but it is what surrounds them that catches your eye. It is too bad that dust layers can't be measured like circles in a tree trunk to determine their age and the age of what lies beneath. Whatever their vintage, the objects on the high shelves, on the floor, and hanging over the balcony railing are all blanketed with the powdery siftings of the years, and you know you are looking at a Sears catalog of everyday living.

Cobwebs drape over long-empty medicine bottles and dusty books. One bottle label is still legible: "Dr. Porter — Antiseptic Healing Oil, discovered by an old railroad surgeon for man and beast." Among the books is *Dr. Porter's Memorandum Book — The Household Surgeon,"* Irvin S. Cobb's *Speaking of Operations,* and a Bible. There is a small book with maps of Europe and the United States, then blank pages, on a few some handwritten tips for treating cuts, burns, bruises, "the itch," frostbite, and so on.

Here and there on the upper walls, faded pink and green wallpaper hangs in strips like tattered cloth. Under one of the high windows, a shelf runs the length of the side wall. On it an eclectic assortment of relics, each wearing its own collection of dust: a man's straw hat, a cow skull, milk cans, a kerosene lamp, dishes.

At the back of the store sits the iron box woodstove that was used to heat the entire story-and-a-half building. Stairs lead up to a small balcony. Worn saddles hang over the railing. Only a little of the brown, painted wood shows through the mantle of silent dust. A milliner once had her shop on the balcony, and ladies lifted their skirts as they climbed the stairs to try on hats. Now a card table and a few chairs sit in the center of the balcony, an unfinished domino game spread out on the table, interrupted how long ago?

During the 1940s, when the Carter men were running the store, Mary Lou's father brought in new types of merchandise: meat, produce, magazines, and newspapers. He was so progressive, he even gave S&H Green Stamps. In some ways, however, he held on to the old ways of running a store. Carter did not believe in electrically cooled Coca Cola boxes. He insisted that his soft drinks be chilled with block ice. Since he had run an ice house in Fort Worth for a number of years, he felt he knew what he was talking about.

Another distinction of the store was its selection of penny candy: peanut butter logs, jawbreakers, suckers, black licorice whips. The store was a favorite stopping-in place for schoolchildren after school, and Mary Lou Wilkins says no one ever convinced her dad that he lost money on that candy.

Her grandfather, "Pop" Carter, slept on the balcony of the store for a number of years. According to the family, Pop was a character, prone to do unconventional things from time to time. The only thing Pop didn't like about sleeping on the balcony was the woodpeckers in the trees outside the high windows of the store. Albert Phillips, the town's postman, and Pop were great friends — even though they argued a lot. Early one morning Phillips decided to help out his friend, so he found a large rock, went to the store, and heaved it at the noisy woodpecker in the tree. Unfortunately, the rock missed the bird but went straight through the window pane, close to the balcony where Pop was sleeping. Later, Pop himself took his own measures to get rid of the woodpeckers by firing a shotgun at them. He missed too, and the shot blew a hole in the side of the store.

A lot of people in town remember Andrew Rose, a bachelor who hung around the store. Rose wore a large black hat and long sleeves, winter and summer, and sported a big, handlebar mustache. Mary Lou said she was always a little afraid of him, for some reason, but that was before he "bought" her small daughter's warts. One day she and her little girl were in the store when Rose asked the child if she would like to get rid of the wart on her hand. Of course she would. Then he said he would buy it for a penny. Mary Lou produced the penny, Rose "grabbed" the wart and, sure enough, in a few days the wart was gone.

Almost everyone in town remembers that the store has been there for as long as he can remember. But no one knows exactly who put it there or who owned all the old things inside.

It is summer, and the yards of old frame houses are filled with mimosa trees, pink, frilly crape myrtle bushes, and garden flowers. By the main road, red and yellow zinnias grow alongside corn. A sign on a fence post reads "Fresh and Sweet Onions — Notary."

The Poolville store has counterparts in dozens of small towns, hanging on to a fragile present, perching on the edge of "gone." About all that holds it together are the cobwebs and a few people's memories.

# 23 | D. B. Lentz Store

*I used to sell a lot of dry goods and sewing machines when women stayed home long enough to make their own clothes.*

— Duncan Lentz

RED ROCK   Stories about how Red Rock acquired its name vary like those about many place names. One account relates how a Mr. Brewer, one of the 1830s settlers, used red rocks to build the tall chimney of his house. Because it could be seen for some distance, it became a landmark. Another story holds that there was a big red rock at the crossroads that led to Austin and other towns. People would say, "Meet me at the red rock and we'll go to town." Nevertheless, there must be some truth in the parts of Red Rock's early history that appear in so many places.

Following the Civil War, Red Rock, like many other towns, saw its share of violence. Much of it was the result of stirred-up agitation between the newly freed former slaves and Southern whites. Carpetbaggers from Austin took full advantage of a difficult transition. Circuit-riding preachers attempted to bring peace and religion to the towns and settlements. Andrew J. "Andy" Potter, "The Fightin' Parson," was one who exemplified "Bible in pocket, gun in hand."

While preaching at nearby Lytton Springs one Sunday, Potter was warned not to come to Red Rock the next Sunday. He replied he had been promised a chicken dinner, and he would come. When he returned, he began his sermon by putting his pair of

*Early in this century, Red Rock had a bank, a lumber yard, two cotton gins, a drugstore, garage, and several mercantile stores. Today, its gently sloping main street is almost empty except for Duncan Lentz's store that sells feed and fertilizer.*

Colt 45s on the pulpit table and announcing, "Now I sent word that I was coming to Red Rock to preach, and I'm gonna preach. But I can shoot too, and anyone who wants a fight and starts one, we'll shoot it out." Potter preached his sermon and got his chicken dinner.

Red Rock's first postmaster in 1870 was Ashley R. Lentz in the original settlement which would come to be called Old Red Rock. A Mr. Hester had a general store in Old Red Rock, and when the railroad came through in 1892, along with the rest of the town, Hester moved to a location closer to the railroad tracks.

By 1906, the town had its first brick building, the bank. As Red Rock grew, becoming a shipping point on the Missouri-Kansas-Texas Railroad, new buildings were erected along the town's gently sloping main street — a lumber yard, hotel, a drugstore, a garage, and Hester's general merchandise store.

About 1907 Hester sold his store to O. B. Lentz, who ran it until 1920, when his son Duncan B. Lentz took over. Two years before Duncan became store owner, however, one of two disastrous fires occurred. The 1918 fire destroyed thirteen Red Rock businesses. Everyone rebuilt, but the town burned again in 1924 — from the Liberty Garage down to the depot. Everyone built again.

Slowly, however, even a stubborn town spirit could not keep the town moving as it once had. The brick bank building collapsed to rubble, and most of the businesses closed.

Today, across the road from the D. B. Lentz store, a grassy lot, once filled with Red Rock businesses, holds memories for only the oldest residents. Next door to the Lentz store, the last grocery store is closing its doors. Nothing is left inside the old drug store to identify it as what it once was. Across the street, the neat little post office building is so new it looks oddly out of place.

On a sweltering summer day in the mid-1980s, octogenarian Duncan Lentz was definitely open for business, no matter what the status of the rest of the town. He had to use a wheelchair and a walker, but that didn't stop him from waiting on customers there to buy feed and fertilizer. That is about all he sells now, except for some hardware, tools, and men's straw hats. The summer heat spreads the quickly identifiable odor out onto the front porch. A cold soft drink plucked from the old red Coca-Cola box with "6¢" on its lid brings a little relief from the weather.

Mr. Lentz says he is getting on in years and doesn't have time to visit. I tell him I understand. I realize he has customers. One man has just carried out two large sacks of feed, calling back over his shoulder that he will be back tomorrow for the rest. During the next hour, I learn that Lentz has some definite ideas on a number of subjects:

"Women in the work force caused all this unemployment. I used to sell a lot of dry goods and sewing machines when women stayed home long enough to make their own clothes."

"People tie up too much money in cars. Kids have to be driven to their friends' houses to play or else they have to have their own cars. If their parents would put all that money in CDs instead of in cars, they'd have more money."

"That fellow Roosevelt killed all the cows and sows and plowed up all the cotton."

"The reason there aren't many burials any more is because cremation is cheaper."

"Home births are growing because the hospitals charge too much."

He tells me he used to sell caskets. "Held one for a woman for eighteen years. When her husband died, she wanted one just like his, so she paid me $110 for it, and I kept it until she needed it. By the time she did, the casket was selling for $2,000. I didn't charge the family any more for it. Just let them have it."

I ask about the rest of Red Rock, and Lentz points to show me where there once stood a doctor's office, lumber yard, and two cotton gins. Then he asks me to go look into the old drug store and see the picture "the hobo painted." It is a nice lake scene, oval-shaped, painted on the drug store wall but framed with a real frame. The colors are still bright.

"It was 1952 when that hobo painted that picture . . . for food," he tells me.

Red Rock isn't very big now — perhaps thirty people actually living in the town, the postmaster says. There are two pretty churches where Fightin' Andy Potter would feel welcome. But the rusting gasoline pumps in front of the grocery store haven't been used in a long, long time. It may have been the hot weather, but very few customers came into the Lentz store for fertilizer or hardware that day.

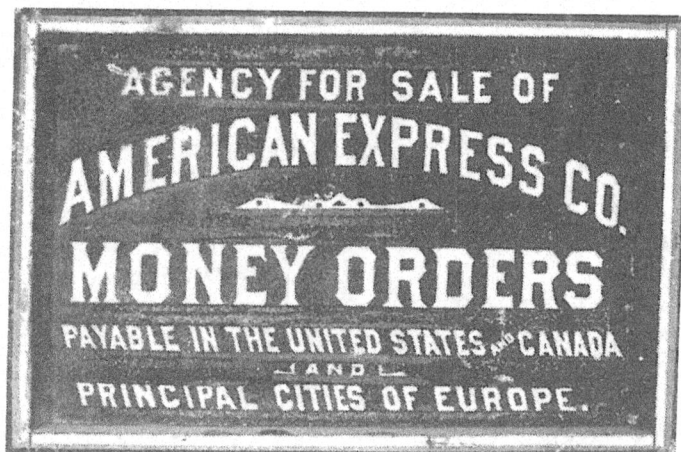

AGENCY FOR SALE OF
AMERICAN EXPRESS CO.
MONEY ORDERS
PAYABLE IN THE UNITED STATES AND CANADA
AND
PRINCIPAL CITIES OF EUROPE.

On Round Top's courthouse square, its big wooden general store dates back to around 1850. The second floor at times was used as a law court, a hotel, and a dance hall.

*In the basement, early storekeepers cooled the dozens of kegs of beer so dear to the hearts of Round Top's German citizens.*

ROUND TOP   Round Top's early settlers planned to lay out the town on Soergel's Hill about two miles from the present town, but the stagecoach line between Austin and Houston passed through the eventual townsite, so they didn't use the hill location. Alvin Soergel's white house had a tower — not round but octagonal-shaped — that was easily visible for miles around from its hilltop. The tower gave Round Top its final name.

The first settlers were Southern planters in the 1840s, many of whom were slaveowners. The rich, black soil in Fayette County produced excellent crops and made the landowners wealthy. Even before the Civil War ended, many of the planters sold much of their land to German immigrants, and before long Round Top was almost entirely a German community.

In 1850 the town had a population of 150, two general mercantile stores, two blacksmith shops, two saloons, a post office, and a stage line that came through three times a week. The town was built primarily around a large square in the center of town, on which the people soon erected a two-story courthouse. That year, a wooden, barn-size building was built, facing the square, to serve as a general store.

The exact lineage of the store isn't known for certain, but two of the earliest owners were Henry Dippel and W. J. Dippel, who ran the store at different times. Both August von Minden and Ernst von Minden were later owners, also operating the store separately. In more recent years, the store has belonged to members of the Schatte family.

The store was put together with wooden pegs and at one time had a bell tower. Over the years, the second floor was used as a law court, a hotel, and a dance hall with a bandstand. Two front entrances on either side of the main entrance led to separate rooms. On one side, Ernst von Minden cut glass for picture frames. This room contains the stairway leading up to the second floor. The other room was once used for giftware that included crepe paper flowers. A tiny room at the back of the first floor was used as a barber shop.

In the basement, early storekeepers cooled the dozens of kegs of beer so dear to the hearts of Round Top's German citizens. It is entirely possible that beer was one of the beverages served at the long, dark wooden bar near the entrance of the store. A few Round Top people remember being served ice cream at the bar while sitting on the wooden stools.

By 1936, Round Top had about 250 people and boasted having three saloons, a drug store, tinsmith shop, cotton gin, blacksmith shop, cigar factory down the road from the big general store, photograph gallery, a doctor, and a shoemaker. Citizens were also proud of their town square, which still had its calaboose, and of the Fourth of July celebrations that had begun in the early 1800s.

It was in 1936 that "W. J. Dippel & Bro. — Dealers in General Merchandise" advertised "Notions, Dress Goods, Cassimers, Domestics, Trimmings, Boots and Shoes, Hats and Caps, Ladies', Misses', and Children's Hats." Their ad also stated that they ". . . pay highest prices for cotton, bacon, lard, chickens, and eggs."

A few of the town's older residents remember the store's busier days. One recalls when you could buy Mother's Oats and receive dishes inside the box as a bonus. Another remembers when the store sold coffins, and a hearse stood at the back of the building. There were days — long ago — when you could buy a three-dip cone of Blue Bell ice cream for a nickel. One native of the town can tell about the road in front of the store when it was dirt and gravel, around 1913. Today it is State Highway 237.

One of the store's owners — in the memories of a number of Round Top people — wouldn't let anyone go upstairs. Older residents remembered dancing up there, and some had never seen it but wanted to, so when Betty Schatte became the store proprietor, one of the first things she did was to have a big party for everyone who wanted to see the second floor.

Betty says that nowadays people come in "mostly just to look," although she sells pots and pans, churns, hardware, and local crafts. You can check out a book in Betty's lending library if you bring another book to exchange for it. On the store shelves, she has on display some of the store's early merchandise: medicines, soap, and some Mother's Oats cereal boxes, the bonus dishes still inside. The old red-and-green Nehi cooler is empty, but you can buy a soft drink from the modern refrigerator.

In the vicinity of the store and throughout Round Top, buildings remain that were new when shoppers in the store were buying plug tobacco, coffee beans, and vinegar from a barrel. The small building next door once served as a movie theater and later a pool hall. Today it is a funeral home. On the road out front, a short distance from the store, the Bauer-Schueddemagen house, built in 1852, is a private residence today. Sitting off the main road not far away, the 1866 Bethlehem Lutheran Church was once the social and religious center for the German townspeople.

Round Top was incorporated in 1865 and remains the smallest incorporated town in Texas with a current population of about eighty-seven. But even with the Houstonians and others moving into the quaint little town, many of its residents still speak in German-flavored accents, and names like Henkel, Schumann, Brau, Schatte, and Nittsche keep Round Top's past alive.

## 25 | Rosston General Store

*Pick cotton on til Doomsday*
*Til Gabriel's trumpet sounds*
*The poor man's curse is cotton*
*At just six cents a pound.*
— "Six Cent Cotton"

ROSSTON   When the Ross brothers came to the little valley on Clear Creek in 1870, they knew they had found the ideal spot for a new town. Plenty of post oak and pecan trees would provide fuel and lumber for the log cabins they would build. Cotton was already being grown in the area, and, in spite of the 1868 Kiowa and Comanche Indian raids, other settlers were coming to the valley in North Texas.

Word of the new settlement had spread through travelers on the Butterfield and Wells Fargo stage lines that ran down the hill east of Rosston and through trail drivers on the John Chisum cattle trail, which passed nearby.

Within a few years, the Ross brothers — O. A., T. A., and W. J. — had built a general merchandise store, a cotton gin, and a mill. By 1873, there were forty-eight people in the village and around 500 in the surrounding area.

Clay, Sam, and Sarah Raney had come to Rosston with their widowed mother in 1868, soon after the Indian raid. On the town's square in 1879 they built the Raney Brothers General Merchandise Store, which is the Rosston General Store today. Originally, the storefront had the familiar Alamo-

*One of the state's most picturesque little stores is in Rosston, north of Denton, where townfolk know their history and are eager to share it with visitors.*

shaped false front with a three-sided overhang covering the front porch. Along one side, a narrow room the length of the store held the caskets for sale. The store carried everything that was available for a settler's needs, even though getting supplies from Gainesville meant a two-day trip, requiring two wagons and four mules during rainy times. The caskets were hauled on bundle wagons that were wider than ordinary wagons.

Clay and Sam sold beef for five cents a pound,

*Around the old box stove, early citizens talked of dining table surgeries, Sam Bass, and the time the circus elephant escaped.*

sugar for thirty-five cents a pound, rice for twenty-five cents a pound, flour at eight dollars for one hundred pounds, and potatoes for twelve and a half cents a pound. Traveling salesmen, or drummers, sold the Raneys all sorts of feminine needs and luxuries such as ribbon, lace, fabric, curling irons, toilet water, and cold cream. For their male customers, they stocked farm tools, horse collars, feed, and long, white cotton-picker sacks that would later be converted into clothing when they were soft and worn.

By 1912, Rosston had four general stores plus Dr. Harper's drug store, a blacksmith shop, and a flour mill. Across the way from the Raney store, J. P. and Caroline Dills ran a hotel. A Baptist church and a Methodist church had been built a few years earlier.

The store changed owners a number of times over the years. George Berry owned it for thirty-three years, and it is now owned by Johnny and Linda Muller. Berry replaced the wooden overhang with a similar tin roof and altered the front profile, but essentially it looks much the same as it did when it was first built. The room where the caskets were stored, along with Christmas toys where the children would not see them, was removed long ago.

These days the store sells most of the needs of Rosston's few remaining residents, including groceries, feed, and even fresh sandwiches for its frequent visitors. In the summer, you can buy fresh blackeyed peas and tomatoes from Rosston gardens; in the fall, pecans from the many old trees in the beautiful valley. But you don't have to look very far to see reminders of an earlier time. The walls are covered with old soft drink signs, and on one hangs the last of the white cotton-picker sacks with its final price tag — $2.19. An old glass display case holds memory-nudging mementos: a paper fan with advertisements for Garrett Snuff and O.J.'s Beauty Lotion, an 1897 arithmetic book, a stereoscope with double-image, and cardboard pictures.

At the back of the store, however, is the old box stove that you wish could talk. Around its warmth, neighbors gathered to talk about the recent flooding of Clear Creek and of the children who could not cross and had to spend the night with friends on the schoolhouse side. Roland Moseley liked to talk about outlaw Sam Bass and his friends, who were said to be hiding out in Cove Hollow under the ridge above the creek. Roland liked to watch the others sitting around the stove lean in to listen as he described his run-in with Sam and three of his boys near the ox-driven mill. Sure he was scared; the gun barrels staring him in the face looked big as saucers, he told them, but since Sam was known as "the gentle bandit" who never killed anyone, Roland tried to remember this and hang on to his nerves.

For a while, the favorite tale around the stove, and for years after, was the one about a circus elephant and a circus ape breaking loose. The elephant broke into Pappy Dills's corn crib, according to the storyteller of the day, and turned over his wagon filled with apples. The ape climbed into the Maughan house, through the window of the baby's room. In later years, G. A. Maughan could tell about the ape with authority: Maughan was the baby the ape lifted out of bed, then dropped when both baby and mother screamed.

Probably J. R. Roach, the last owner of the Rosston cotton gin, would be the one to recite a poem printed in the *Gainesville Register*. It was a favorite of all the cotton farmers. Listeners appreciated the lines of "Six Cent Cotton" as J. R. would repeat its lines from memory:

> To you, my fellow farmers,
> I sing a brand new song,
> Although my tune is doubtful
> And often slightly wrong.
>
> The words, however awkward,
> With simple truth are croned,
> 'Tis about our raising cotton
> At just six cents a pound.
>
> Set out the old sour buttermilk,
> We'll drink to all the land,
> Make some good brand coffee,
> Quite strong enough to stand.

Oh, make a yellow corn dodger,
And bake it devilish brown,
I'm a man who raises cotton
At just six cents a pound.

March on to picking cotton,
Strap on a duckin' sack
With cotton burrs hitting at your face
And another one at your back.

Pick cotton on til Doomsday
Til Gabriel's trumpet sounds
The poor man's curse is cotton
At just six cents a pound.

Bring out the old jeans breeches,
Never too late to mend,
And put a patch, both broad and wide,
Across the gable end.

And write across the patch work
In letters big and round
I am a Man who raises cotton
At just six cents a pound.

Sometimes the group would be joined by a circuit-riding preacher such as Hamn Branch. Reverend Branch always liked to sit in the chair with the leather strip seat, and he often held his Bible and his saddle bag (which carried a clean, white shirt) in his lap.

Talk frequently turned to illnesses, injuries, and deaths in town, of Dr. Harper and Dr. Johnson, kitchen and dining table surgeries, doses of quinine and calamel, and burials in the Rosston Cemetery. It was a close, caring little community — and still is.

Each July, Rosston celebrates Sam Bass Day — "just an excuse for everyone to get together," one resident says. The Rosston General Store is the center of all the festivities and visiting, along with the fire station across what was the town's square. The store is Rosston's only remaining business. Lots of former residents come back for the picnic, parade, mule pull, gunfight competition, and square dance.

Undoubtedly, many of the visitors on Sam Bass Day take time to go up the winding, dusty road from the store to the cemetery alongside the white, steepled Methodist church. Their forebears are there, names on the markers the same names as the visitors and their families in Rosston today: Harper, Ford, Muller, Berry, Mosely, Kelley, Dills, and, of course, Raney. After walking among the quiet graves, perhaps they come back to the store and sit around the stove on one of the old tractor seat stools or on the wooden funeral home bench. Some probably stand out on the front porch and maybe talk about how the price of cotton has changed over the years. Early-day Rosston farmers wouldn't believe the price today.

Rosston holds its memories and traditions in a strong but gentle grasp, and you feel the closeness of its people every minute you are there. If the Ross brothers could return, they would be pleased with their town, and the Raney brothers would be grateful to all the people who are taking care of their store.

# 26 W. J. Dube Store

*Men sat on the bench in front and whittled away at it and argued Scripture a lot.*

— Ted Graham

THE GROVE   Sometimes "progress" can almost kill a little town — if a world war can be considered progress. Although it brought prosperity to some places, when the government built Fort Hood, it took away from the farmers around The Grove some 322 square miles of prime farm land. Years before, the railroad had laid its tracks ten miles to the north. Then, State Highway 36 was built, not through The Grove but to the east, so that the only way anyone could know there was a town there was by seeing the tall, Lutheran church steeple.

Fort Hood brought new life to surrounding towns like Killeen, Temple, and Gatesville, but the highway linked them to each other and left The Grove sitting all by itself among the live oaks between Owl Creek and the Leon River. By the 1950s, construction of Belton Dam took even more land and left even more farmers with no place to plow.

A few people had arrived in this region before the 1870s, preceding the first real settlement. Military personnel used the same path they followed to bring supplies to Fort Gates, located several miles north of The Grove. Kernels of corn, dropped from the supply wagons, took root and grew along the way, and the road came to be known as the Old Corn Road. Parts of this route followed the main road through The Grove.

The largest group of settlers were the Wends, immigrants from Central Europe who left because of religious persecution. They came to Texas, founding Lutheran churches in such settlements as Serbin, New Ulm, Industry, and Warda. Among these

*The W. J. Dube Store in The Grove, northwest of Temple, today serves as a store museum where visitors can easily imagine they are shopping for the same items their grandmothers did.*

*Ted Graham helped build the store and remembers when men sat on the wooden bench outside the store "and argued Scripture a lot."*

Wends were the names of Winkler, Dube, Schkade, Drosche, Symm, and Hohle.

The Grove post office was established in 1874, and the little town grew rapidly around the twenty-eight-foot well that had been dug by Uncle Jim Whitmore. Surrounding the well were several general stores, Durham's candy kitchen, Glass's mule barn, Holcome and Adams's blacksmith shop, a lumber yard, cotton gin, and two barber shops. The Grove also had a school, several churches, doctors, a coffin maker, and two barbers.

One of the earliest general stores in The Grove was near the well in a little wooden building run by August Schkade and W. J. Dube. When Schkade died, Dube married his widow. In 1917 he built a block-long, red-brick façade store on the main road in the center of town. The two-story adjoining build-

*Built in 1917, the store, post office, and bank were the polestar of the little community.*

—Moody Anderson

ing was designed for a post office and an upstairs occupant. For years the upstairs was used as a doctor's office and later as a barber shop. One corner inside the store was enclosed to serve as the Planters State Bank that opened in September of 1917 with a capital stock of $10,000.

The store became The Grove's heartbeat. Dube started every business day by 5:00 A.M., winding his Linz Brothers clock that he had won from the Dallas jewelers for selling a lot of something — in later years he couldn't remember what. Shoppers could visit around the big woodstove or wander the long aisles where they would find everything from cowbells to coffins. Dube sold dry goods, groceries, harnesses, patent medicines, brooms — anything anyone needed.

In front of the store, the dirt road was often filled with Huey Dixon's cattle being driven to market. Ted Graham, who helped build the store, remembers that "sometimes the road was so crowded with wagons filled with cotton waiting for the gin that you couldn't find a place to tie up your horse."

From the day the store opened, men sat on the long wooden bench in front and whittled away at it as they talked. Finally, the bench had to be reinforced with metal bands to hold it together. What did they talk about? Ted says they "argued Scripture a lot." Not too surprising, considering there were Baptist, Methodist, Church of Christ, and Lutheran churches in The Grove.

They also may have discussed whether or not it really was Sam Bass who appeared in town one day during the 1870s. Ted's grandfather, W. J. Graham, said it was. Graham had unknowingly served the gunfighter dinner, and Bass asked him what he would do if Sam Bass asked him for his money.

"I'd tell him to go to hell," Graham told him.

"Well, I'm Sam Bass," the visitor said.

"If you are, then that's a different matter."

Later, a gun was found in a nearby pasture with the initials "S. B." carved on it.

Excitement around the store during the town's early years followed the script of many a western movie. Four shootouts in front, and in 1927 a bank robbery that left the Planters State Bank minus $1,022. The robbers were caught, but again in 1932 the bank lost money when an employee embezzled a large amount of cash by keeping two sets of books. These events, together with the economic depression of the time, led to the bank's voluntary liquidation in 1932.

A brighter part of The Grove's colorful past was the annual Doolittle Championship Rodeo held each July 4, beginning in 1928. Austin Doolittle, the town character, brought hundreds of people to The Grove for this event. Another annual episode, dear to the hearts of the community's young people, was the New Year's Eve disassembling of Doolittle's buggy and assembling it again on top of Dube's store.

During the 1940s and 1950s, townspeople would gather at the school to watch movies projected on the side of the building. However, after World War II, while the store continued to serve the town, many people moved away or did not come back from their wartime activities.

When Dube decided to sell the store, he sold it to Jim Gilbert, who ran it for a short while before selling it to John Graham. Graham and his wife Ruby, the postmaster, ran it in the best tradition of country storekeepers for thirteen years. Graham continued to wind Dube's clock, sold red soda pop to the children in town, closed the store for a funeral when a neighbor died, and tried to keep the fancy brass grillwork and footrail in front of the bank teller's cage free of the dust that drifted in from the dirt road in front.

During these years, Ruby ran the post office from the bank enclosure where she could also watch the store. She used the room built for the post office as a kitchen, where she prepared lunch for John and anyone else who happened to be around at noontime.

Shortly before he closed the store for good, John Graham sold his Linz Brothers clock to a local man for twenty-five dollars. Postmaster Eula Mae Graham Kindler, his daughter, was saddened by the sale and cannot explain why her father let it go. "Perhaps he didn't know either," she says.

In 1972 Moody Anderson, history buff and antique dealer from Austin, bought the store and post office building from Graham. He also owns the little wooden building next door, once another store, and the old blacksmith shop next to it. He opens the store on weekends for special occasions or for groups, and he allows Eula Mae to show it to visitors with a special interest in his treasures which also fill the blacksmith shop.

It probably isn't an exaggeration to say that Anderson has collected at least one of every item ever sold in a general store during the first quarter of this century and has placed it on display in his store. Although nothing is for sale, unless you look closely and see a little rust, a yellowed label, a bit of dust here and there, you can easily imagine yourself as a customer fifty or more years ago.

Here are the glass-fronted counter bins where beans, rice, dried peas, and other staples were stored. On a counter sit flour sacks that once held popular brands of their day: Quality Mills, Pioneer Flour Mills, Washburn Crossing, Angel Food, Purasnow. There are corn meal sacks from Martha White and Victor Mills; soda pop bottles (you remember Uncle Jo and Nehi); coffees (MJB, Red & White, 1869, Mi Boy, Bright & Early); and all the medicines that people once believed in: 666 Malerial, Thacher's Cough Syrup, Black Draught, Dr. Caldwell's Laxative, and Cardui ("has helped women for 50 years"). Nowadays, you can hardly find Star tobacco or Satin cigarettes (15¢). Or how about Finch's Detroit Special overalls ("Wear Like a Pig's Nose") and "Star Brand Shoes Are Better"? Anderson also found some Big Berthe hair dressing and Gainsborough hair nets among other countless items that mirror what people needed and wanted and used during the early 1900s.

Next to the bank enclosure, a colorful wooden Indian guards the teller's cage against any further wrongdoing. By the stove, a wooden bench made by the Future Farmers of America from Flat, up the road, still offers visitors a resting place.

There is more. Back rooms hold old farm tools, and one niche shows what burials required a hundred years ago. At one side an early-day embalming table, close by a black velvet-covered casket embellished with a silver plate reading "Rest In Peace." In a wooden box, a child's coffin, made in The Grove — white, lined with white, lacy fabric and adorned with a silver medallion. At one side, a small enameled sign, perhaps from a mortician's office: "Preserve Every Grave."

Outside, sitting on the old, whittled-up bench, I can hear the occasional firing of heavy artillery at Fort Hood — a reminder of the kind of progress that reduced The Grove's population to the present-day number of sixty-five. Still standing outside the post office is John Graham's faded gasoline pump, which he only filled once with its ten-gallon limit because customers bought on credit and "weren't too good about paying up." At the end of the building, the wooden stairs that lead up to the office where Dr. Collins once had his office are gray with the shimmer of forgotten days. On a morning with no one around the store except the few remaining residents who come to get their mail, I wish I could have been in The Grove when Austin Doolittle had his rodeo and W. J. Dube's clock was still ticking in his store.

# 27 | Welcome General Store

*When German settlements such as Industry and New Ulm were full, families moved northward to a site they named Welcome. The first general store was built by John Reichle in 1890, and by 1900 the town had a cotton gin, blacksmith shop, creamery, molasses factory, and a saw mill. Here farmers weigh cotton at the scales outside the store, and a traveling peddler shows his wares.*

*A board stretched across the hitching posts in front of the store provided a resting place to watch cotton bales being weighed on the scales by the tree.*

WELCOME    According to one story, Welcome was named by one of the first German settlers who came to Austin County in 1852. J. F. Schmidt selected the name because "everything — forest, field, meadows, and flowers — seem to give us a friendly welcome." A later story credits the name to the hospitality of Welcome residents. When travelers stopped to water their horses and to rest, they thanked the townspeople as they were leaving and were told, "You're welcome!"

To the south, other settlements were rapidly filling up with German newcomers. When land was all taken around Industry and New Ulm, families moved their wagons northward through the rolling hills to the site of Welcome. They carried names that would be heard in this region for years to come: Vogelsang, Boeker, Schelling, Kruse, Huebner, Schmidt, and Reichle. By 1871, a post office was established with Henry Meyer as postmaster, followed by Christopher Schmidt in 1875. The Germans built

a Lutheran church on the main road and a school on the banks of Pecan Creek.

In 1890 John Reichle erected a white, two-story, barn-shaped general merchandise store on the main road. It also contained the Welcome post office. Around the turn of the century, the town had a bank across the road from the store, a cotton gin, blacksmith shop, creamery, tin shop, molasses factory, and saw mill. During those years, a small hospital was operated by a German doctor whose treatments included sweating out fevers and blood-letting. No one could ever explain the reason, but the doctor committed suicide.

Reichle's store carried all of the little community's needs and a few modern luxuries like matches and soap. Goods arrived by wagon, often pulled by oxen. Traveling peddlers used a team of horses to pull their wagons, loaded with colorful calico, gingham, outing, velvet, lace, ribbon, braid, thread, and Putnam Fadeless Dyes and Tints. One such wagon was designed so that store owners could examine merchandise from outside the wagon and make their selections. A heavy tarp could be lowered over the sides, protecting the wagon's contents as the peddler rode from town to town. Lucky was the rural housewife who might be at the store when the peddler's wagon arrived. Seeing the newest fabrics and picturing how they would look made up into new dresses and bonnets added extra pleasure to getting away from the farm and the monotony of cooking, cleaning, and child-tending.

In Welcome, as in all small towns, men used the store as a place to meet and talk about the price of crops and to exchange the latest news about their family and friends. A board stretched across the hitching posts in front of the store provided a resting place to watch cotton bales being weighed on the scales by the tree. The board was replaced in the 1930s by a chain that the younger men found just as convenient when they brought their new cars to the store to fill up with gasoline, one of the more recent needs the store offered for sale.

The 1900 storm that destroyed Galveston, 100 miles to the south of Welcome, also destroyed the town's church and probably damaged the store. Whenever Reichle rebuilt the store, he replaced it with a one-story, twin-gabled structure, the one that stands today.

After Reichle died, the store was run by Mr. and

Mrs. Henry Schmidt and later by Sanford Schmidt, by now a familar Welcome name. The most recent owners have been Evelyn and the late Clemons Faist.

Today, no young people around the store talk about the horse races between Welcome and Industry nor the Saturday night dance on the big wooden platform near the store. The interior of the store has been modernized, but there are still reminders of the years when Farm Road 109 in front was an unpaved link between Industry and Brenham. The counter and stools remain from the days when you could buy a dish or a cone of ice cream. The old broom rack still holds new brooms; a kerosene pump hasn't been used for many a day, but the egg candler still as-

sures customers that their eggs are fine. Underneath the glass in the front door and the logo showing which credit cards the store accepts, the original lock and key secure the store at night.

On the front porch, a long, straight-backed church pew, aged to a gray sheen, invites customers to sit and talk a while. At one side of the store, a giant tree could easily have held one end of the chain where the local boys sat to swap stories.

Only about 150 people live around Welcome today, but the big limestone Lutheran church which overlooks the highway and John Reichle's store still make the descendants of the Vogelsangs and Schellings and Schmidts — as well as travelers — always feel welcome.

# 28 Gene Jansing's Grocery

*In its own way, the store is a constant for the people in Westphalia, like the church.*

WESTPHALIA  Westphalia is the kind of place travelers often discover by accident. Located outside of Temple on the shortest state highway in the state, Westphalia was settled by German Catholics from the province of this name in what is now West Germany.

In 1879 Theodore Rabroker, Westphalia's first settler, was traveling in two mule-drawn wagons from Tarrant County, where he had been living with his family. They had come to Texas from Iowa and were en route to Frelsburg in South Texas. Stopping in Falls County, Rabroker envisioned a Catholic community amidst the shoulder-high grass on the fertile prairie. After establishing his own home there, he invited German families from Frelsburg to come buy 270-acre homesteads. Only German Catholics were urged to come, and soon the area was populated by industrious, thrifty families with names such as Hoelscher, Jansing, Glass, Schneider, Frei, Buxkemper, and Boeselt.

The community's initial goal was to build a church and a school. Their first 1883 church was destroyed by a storm, but in 1895 Westphalia parishioners built the twin-towered Church of the Visitation, facing their cemetery. One of the school's first teachers was Stephen Geiser, in 1881. Geiser opened Westphalia's first place of business in 1890, a general merchandise store.

Westphalia grew and prospered as the hardworking German farmers garnered crops from the rich soil. At one time the town had two cotton gins to

*When a highway was rerouted, stores often found their fronts becoming their back entrances as in Jansing's store in Westphalia. Today's back door was the original front of the store.*

handle the abundant cotton crops. Around 1931, however, people began moving away due to the lack of land for further development. Still, in 1933, when the church celebrated its fiftieth anniversary, a number of businesses were operating, including Gausemeir and Fuelder Groceries and Drugs, the Gottschalk Brothers Cotton Gin, Herman Hoelscher Dry Good and Notions, Greener's Garage, Zeig's Tin Shop, and Kleypas Grocer ("We Handle Your Produce.").

Whether or not the Stephen Geiser store was the same as Gene Jansing's Grocery today cannot be confirmed, but Charles Kleypas was the owner when Gene went to work in the store back in the

*The front of the Jansing store today faces State Highway 320, northeast of Temple.*

1940s, and Westphalia's first store that Geiser ran could not have been more vital to the community than is Gene's store today.

Jansing is a descendant of one of Westphalia's first settlers. When his store was built — at whatever time, some say about 1907 — its Alamo-shaped false front faced what was then the main road. When the state built Highway 320 behind the store, the back door became the front door, and automobiles, more often than horses and wagons, began pulling up to the store. Today, it is one of three remaining businesses, including another old grocery store

*The old doors to Jansing's store tell customers which bread is sold inside.*

across the road and a meat market.

Much of the store's history can be read on the outside of the building. Across the screen doors on the original front side, the metal Rainbo bread signs are rusty with age, and the doors themselves evidence the years of Westphalians coming and going. Dozens of schoolchildren and other visitors have written their names and opinions around the doors. Signs, both faded and new on the outside walls, tell customers what they can buy inside: to quench a thirst, Barq's Root Beer, Big Red, and almost any kind of beer. Gene also sells seed, feed, hardware, and all kinds of groceries.

Inside, a clothes line strung almost the length of the store holds hand-lettered signs announcing other good buys around Westphalia: "Rock, sand, gravel and top soil," "Heavy-duty post hole diggers," along with bulletins of interest to everyone in town. The most important one this day says "No Hamburgers August 15." Local folks need no further explanation. Gene's Friday hamburgers, served in the adjoining room, are famous. On August 15, Gene's birthday, he adds to his sign "Everybody Welcome," and he knows to be prepared. On that occasion he always throws a birthday party — brisket, beans, Westphalia noodles, and beer — all free. Between 500 and 600 guests came to the party in 1986; the population of Westphalia hovers around 324.

The store's floor rolls and buckles under your feet so that now and then you are sure that it is moving. Every corner holds evidence of the store's age. In one, an enclosed stairway leads up to the storage loft and is cluttered with cardboard boxes; on the wooden handrail is accumulated grime from all the hands that have held onto it over the years. On a corner wall, cobwebby dust covers cast iron and tin discards that couldn't dry up and blow away: two cowbells, a branding iron, block ice tongs, a string dispenser, bits of harness, a tin cup. No paint has touched the pressed tin ceiling design, perhaps since the store first opened. Rust shows through what may have been a layer of pale blue paint. On the floor, open post office boxes are used today for newspapers that people subscribe to and pick up at the store.

In its own way the store is a constant for the people in Westphalia, like the church. Schoolchildren drop by early each morning perhaps to buy notebook paper and to visit with Gene, who makes sure they leave on time to beat the tardy bell. After school, older children drop by to visit and play pinball, but Gene scoots them out to be home on time for dinner. Sundays, he opens up after 8:00 Mass, then closes at 11:00 for church and Sunday dinner. At 1:00, he opens up again. Whenever he is open, whatever day, anyone who wishes may play the upright piano in the next room, and usually someone does while others gather around and sing.

Sitting on one of the worn-smooth stools in front of the bar, a visitor can rest a foot on the pipe railing and visit with Gene's hamburger cooks or townspeople who drop in. Not surprisingly, their last names sound familiar: Hoelscher, Frei, Gudat. Helen Hoelscher, Elsie Frei, and Florine Gudat cook in the little kitchen off the community room, working around the big, square, oak table. Like other things in the store, the table's age is uncertain.

They want to know if I have seen their church, pride sounding in their voices. I agree it is beautiful.

They aren't sure about the exact age of the store either, but they love working there. Everyone in town comes in regularly, especially on Friday nights when old and young come for hamburgers. "Sometimes we cook 200 to 300."

Gene Jansing's store is the town's fingerprint, and even though many natives move away from Westphalia, they return for the annual October homecoming — and they all come by the store. Helen Hoelscher says, "I wouldn't live anywhere else for nothin'." A lot of her neighbors feel the same way.

# 29 | Martha's Country Store

*Do you remember "Red Wing" and "Jesus Loves Me"? I used to play those.*
— *"The Last Grandmother"*

WINCHESTER   You wouldn't think many people would come to shop in a little country store located some two blocks distant from the main road, especially when it is a farm-to-market road several miles from any town. But they did, and they still do, even though nowadays Martha Goebel sells only chips, soft drinks, and sausage from Taylor.

In early spring, the road between Smithville and Winchester is banked knee-deep in yellow wildflowers. The lane to Martha Goebel's store and her house where she has lived for more than ninety years is shaded with huge pecan trees, live oaks, and hackberries that her brothers planted over fifty years ago. Alongside the lane, Pin Oak Creek is hidden by thick trees. The big barn that Martha's father built stands, grayed and splintered. Under a large tree across the road, the little outhouse sits with its half-open door tilting on its hinges.

Martha is sitting in a big wooden rocker on the front porch of her home when I drive up. I open the metal gate of her fence and join her. As I sit down in the weathered wooden swing, she fingers her apron.

"My children get after me for always having my apron on," she says with a little laugh. I tell her she looks fine.

Martha likes to talk about her store and the days when she and husband Rhyne kept it open, even on Sundays (after church, of course). She remembers when Rhyne and her brothers built the little store about 1933 in the board and batten method of vertical wood strips from lumber they had cut in their saw mill. They painted it green and added an overhang that sheltered the kerosene pump and later gasoline pumps.

*Martha Goebel's store hasn't been on the main road between Smithville and Winchester since the 1930s, but people in the area all know where this true "country store" is located.*

At first the store was on "the main road" down by the bridge at the foot of the lane, she tells me. The day Rhyne and "the moving men" put the store on wheels to move it up beside the house where Martha grew up, Pin Oak Creek was overflowing its banks.

"Oh, I thought they would never get it up the lane to here," Martha recalls, her words colored with the Slavic-German accents of her Wendish-German ancestors.

I follow her through the store's narrow, double doors, darkened to a deeper shade of green above the doorknob by the hundreds of hands that have opened them during the past half century. She moves slowly along the narrow aisle that runs the store's length, apologizing for her slightly bent body. I ask a lot of questions, and the answers come quickly. I am not the first writer to visit and be interested in her store and her life.

The long, narrow shelves attached to the out-

*Martha's Wendish ancestors settled in this part of Central Texas, and she still speaks in their German-Slavic accents.*

side of the big wooden counter? "Oh, those were filled with fresh vegetables, eggs, that kind of thing."

My eye catches an enormous white, wooden icebox with mirrored doors. "Rhyne bought that down in West Point for twenty-five dollars." She laughs and gestures toward the box, forefinger and thumb held together. "I once had a *whole* beef in there."

She wants to sit down "so my back'll feel better." No tone of complaint in her voice. She selects a chair in front of the icebox, near a tall, barrel-size stove. It came out of an old school building, she tells me, and at various times has burned wood, coal, even electricity.

I ask about her early education. "We spoke only Wendish at the table," she says. "I had to start school in Winchester when I was seven to learn to speak English and German."

Does she still know any Wendish? She laughs her deep, rolling laugh and sings a little song for me about two mosquitoes behind a barn. How did she get to her school in Winchester, three miles away? "Walked — most of the time — except when I caught a ride on a donkey a friend of mine up on the hill owned. She and I were about the same age. Or sometimes I rode behind my brother on his horse. One morning I remember . . ." She laughs at the memory. "I saw a *big* dark cloud coming. I ran all the way to school from the creek down there. It usually took an hour, and I got there in twenty minutes!"

I want to know about her parents. Although Martha's knowledge of her ancestry is sketchy, her parents Carl and Maria Schultze no doubt were among the hundreds of Wendish and German immigrants who came to Texas in the middle and late 1800s from a region that is now East Germany. They settled in this part of South Central Texas in Serbin, New Ulm, Industry, Warda, and Lott, where Martha was born.

Suddenly, she reaches behind her chair and opens one of the icebox doors. When she withdraws her hand, she holds a beautiful, illuminated birth certificate, in a frame and written in German. She smiles at my look of surprise and admiration.

I ask about Rhyne, and later when she shows me a picture of the tall, handsome man, I better appreciate what she has told me. Rhyne lived across the meadow, and they married in 1913 when Martha was twenty. He died in 1957, and she has run the store mostly by herself ever since. They were married in St. Michael's Lutheran Church in Winchester.

"We rode in a surrey to the church from here, then came back and had the reception in the house my parents lived in" — the house next door where she and Rhyne also lived and reared their children.

"Rhyne raised cotton," she says, "and one year the harvest was so small, we barely had enough for one bale. That was the year he began selling Ford cars." She gestures a wide circle. "Right here. He was *good* at it."

Near the door sits Rhyne's dust-covered, roll-top desk, the writing edge worn from the hours he must have spent there, recording sales and inventory. On a nearby shelf, two of his hats, yellowed with age, serve as silent reminders of Martha's handsome husband.

She pushes herself up slowly from the chair. There is something in a box on top of an old glass display case that she wants to show me. I reach it for her, and she pulls out a plastic-covered, yellowed grocery ad. She says it was made especially for them in 1937 by a grocery salesman.

"He wanted a name for this place, and I told him it didn't have one, so he just made one up."

Across the top of the ad, "Goebelsville," underneath, items for sale in the store: dog food — six cans for 25¢; tomatoes — three for 25¢; salmon — 19¢ a can; Oxydol — 20¢; Octagon soap — five bars for 19¢; three pounds of Pillsbury flour — 15¢.

Martha needs to sit down again, so she goes back to her chair in front of the icebox. Around us, faded clutter, boxes on long shelves, once filled with groceries. Across the back of the store, dusty Christmas lights strung across the aisle. She follows my eye. "I turn them on at Christmas," she assures me.

On the wall is a 1913 calendar and a hand-carved, wooden paddle of some sort on a hook. No,

Martha says, guess again. Rhyne carved it for opening large cardboard boxes of merchandise, she tells me proudly.

Has she ever traveled much? Oh yes, to Port Arthur, to Houston, even Arizona once, but she likes best to remember riding in her father's Oakland car on her first trip to Austin to see the circus. She didn't like going back though. "It changed too much."

Talk turns to more family members. She lost a son a few years back. "My puppy misses him so." There is pain in her voice. "He lays on the porch and just listens for his master."

Before I leave, she guides me through her home, filled with possessions from the years. Standing before her old organ, she asks, "Do you remember 'Red Wing' and 'Jesus Loves Me'? I used to play those." I tell her I remember.

Back in the store, I ask about a faded photograph inside one of the old glass cases. In it, a beautiful young girl, obviously dressed for a special occasion, smiles at the photographer. "Yah!" she answers, "That was me in my confirmation dress. Someone the other day said I was 'a good-looking chick'!" She was.

I ask more about her family: two sons in Smithville, two nieces not far away, and a granddaughter in New York City.

"You know, Dan Rather," she says casually. I'm confused. "Jean Rather. She's my granddaughter.

She married Dan Rather."

I believe her but have to note that the subject came up by chance.

She gets up and reaches under the counter, producing an often-folded newspaper clipping. It is — of course — a story about her with a photo of her and her famous grandson-in-law.

"He's a fine man," she tells me. "After he married my granddaughter, he called her mother and thanked her for having such a fine daughter!"

The weather is warm. I look around and know I can buy a cool soft drink or some potato chips or Taylor sausage. But it isn't what Martha sells — or doesn't sell — that makes it hard to leave.

We walk down the narrow aisle, past the big icebox and the old stove, out the double doors to the store steps. I notice that the last prices on the gasoline pumps outside read thirty-nine and forty-nine cents a gallon. Martha doesn't remember exactly when she sold the last gasoline, but she recalls pumping coal oil from the kerosene pump many times.

I have to say goodbye and leave her standing on the steps in front of the still-sturdy little store that Rhyne and her brothers built. She smiles her soft smile and waves to me. I think of Dan Rather's story about her that the La Grange newspaper ran. He called her "the last grandmother," one of a disappearing breed of women. Certainly, she is the last one who will run a country store by Pin Oak Creek where every spring the yellow wildflowers bloom.

# 30   "Closed"

*Dust lies like dingy gauze over counters, shelves, floor, lamps, pans — everything.*

## A. Sherley and Brothers General Merchandise, Anna (Collin County)

Across the road from the railroad tracks, A. Sherley & Brothers store sits, closed and quiet except for the rackety slapping of a rusty paint sign against the old red brick. On the building's side, giant, fading letters — BEECHNUT SLICED BACON — are barely legible through the vines that shroud the building. The wind that flaps the sign ruffles leaves of Virginia creeper, a heavy network of vines wrapped so tightly that the side door is permanently sealed.

It is a lonely place. If it were Sunday, people would be standing on the lawn of the nearby white, steepled church. Beyond the railroad tracks, Main Street is almost deserted, most of the old buildings empty and in various stages of death. But you only have to step inside the front door of the Sherley general store to imagine what the town was like when the Sherley brothers opened their business in 1893 here in Anna.

The town had been laid out in 1883 with a population of twenty. Before long, it had a Baptist church, a steam grist mill, and two general stores. The Sherley store made three. Andrew Sherley not only helped run the store but served as ticket agent for the Houston and Texas Central Railroad. Later, he would be Anna's second postmaster. By 1900, Anna had over 400 people, and the town was still growing. People were calling the new century "the

*No longer open to visitors or shoppers, the Andrew Sherley store in Anna, north of McKinney, served its townsfolk for 91 years, not only as a general mercantile store but also as a funeral parlor and a garage.*

Age of Optimism."

Now inside the Sherley store that was closed in 1984, I try to imagine it filled with activity: long-skirted women, their hair twisted and piled high on their heads; black-stockinged children. In many ways the store could have been suspended in time for much more than a few years. My eyes sweep around the lower floor and realize that here, among the dusty clutter, is every conceivable implement, household furnishing, and luxury known to those early-century shoppers: spitoons, an organ, a chest-high phonograph, a wall telephone, slim Coca-Cola bottles, a set of white, painted doll furniture.

Grayed, wooden floors have buckled with age so that some of the furnishings on the floor tilt at unnatural angles, giving the room a further sense of fantasy. Steep stairs at the back lead to a small balcony with more items the Sherleys sold and to rooms I would see later — and never forget.

Two faded wool buggy robes hang over the brown wooden railing. I touch the stair rail, and my fingers sink through velvety layers of the years. I climb the stairs and look down at the lower floor, see again shoppers exchanging pieces of their lives as they bought shoes, clothing, groceries, some of them tenant farmers, charging their purchases against the fall cotton crop.

Behind one counter, almost to the ceiling, small drawers hold medicines and assorted merchandise. Each drawer has a small porcelain knob with hand-painted letters to identify its contents. I consider how similar the general stores were to our modern supermarkets, only the farmer I see in my imagination could not buy two packets of garden seed for a nickel today. Nor could the woman at the foot of the stairs replace her shawl for fifty cents, her bead purse for fifty-nine cents — 1900 price tags.

The scene fades away. Now only silence in the store. Dust lies like dingy gauze over counters,

shelves, floor, lamps, pans — everything. I move through a balcony door to the rooms where the mortuary was operated. Through another door to a small niche, the embalming room. In the shadows, at the end of the room, two coffins rest, draped with dust, one with a carved wooden lid, once white, now gray; another, all-copper except for the glass face covering, designed for someone who had died of a contagious disease. (Still, morticians often contracted the diseases.)

Do I want to see an old burial gown? Of course. In its original box, labeled "Woman's Burial Robe — Dallas Coffin Company," the dress lies in its earthly resting place, once white, now yellowed satin and silk, the front and high neck covered with yellowed lace. I think of *Great Expectations* and Miss Havisham in her yellowed wedding dress, waiting for someone who never comes. I am totally immersed in fantasy when my guide, Andrew Sherley's granddaughter, suggests we see another room.

Down the steep stairs to the outside I see another door and another building joined to the store — the combination carriage house, blacksmith shop, and storage room for wagons and other vehicles and for the wooden boxes in which the coffins upstairs were shipped.

When the carriage room door is opened, I take an involuntary quick breath even before I step in. The dank smell and feel of the cavernous room sweeps over and past me in a ghostly draft. I move into the room and look up at the darkened rafters, where slivers of daylight sift through. Gradually, I identify the outlines of what I am looking at and realize that this is real, however dreamlike it seems. Rusted plows, once new and for sale in the store, rest in a neat, straight line where they were placed who knows how many years ago. A 1924 Lincoln coupe, once someone's pride; a 1918 motorized hearse, its glass windows surrounded with ornate carving; an old blue pickup of uncertain years; a horse-drawn hearse with heavy brass fixtures, shining still against the black, painted sides; a wagon, and — hanging from the rafters — an ancient, black buggy, its huge, round wheels suspended in the air. If they begin moving, I won't be surprised.

I feel like an intruder, curiously waking some sleeping participants from another time, pulling back their dusty shrouds to poke and wonder. I have the feeling that if my companion and I speak too loudly, the spell will be broken, and everything — dust, dampness, buggy, hearses, wagon, plows — will all vanish.

Walking over the hard, irregular dirt floor, I examine more things covered with the monotone of age: a big woodstove (the room's only source of heat, probably, except for the blacksmith's forge in the center of the room), an early road grader, an early washing machine, a row of small school desks with

One of several former stores in Texas that have earned historical markers, the Stewards Mill store served as a post office, telephone exchange, and possibly as a bank. Today, it is overgrown and almost forgotten in Freestone County, north of Fairfield.

On the Stewards Mill back porch, an old rusting red kerosene pump sits anchored to the floor where it filled hundreds of containers over the years.

ornate iron sides and inkwells. Who said, "We bring to travel our own pasts"? I think of these words now.

I take a final, quick look before we leave. From the rafters a hanging sign reads "Fort Smith Wagons," under it the wooden coffin boxes. Andrew Sherley's granddaughter opens the door, and a breeze stirs the whispering dust inside. Outside, only the whacking of the rusted paint sign breaks the silence.

have been removed, but a visit to the Fairfield Museum eight miles to the south will give you a glimpse into the kinds of things the store once sold.

## Stewards Mill Store
(Freestone County)

Washington Steward had a grist mill at this site before it was a store. His was the only such mill between Houston and Dallas. People came from great distances and camped out, waiting to have their wheat or corn ground. After the mill was burned by Union troops during the Civil War, Steward rebuilt in 1867. The store served as a post office, telephone exchange, possibly as a bank, and general store for many years. In 1964 it earned a Texas Historical Survey Committee medallion. Today, the store is closed and overgrown with tangled vines, empty of the whiskey barrels, coffins, nails, and buggy springs it once sold to East Texans in Freestone County.

For years the store was kept open as a store-museum by Mr. and Mrs. Frank Bragg and Mrs. L. G. Daugherty of nearby Fairfield. Mrs. Bragg and Mrs. Daugherty were great-great-granddaughters of Washington Steward. The present owner is Ann Steward Waddell. All of the contents of the store

## Morris Ranch Store
(Gillespie County)

When Francis Morris from New York state came to Central Texas in the late 1800s, he only intended to raise a few race horses in a warm climate. By 1899, one of the coldest winters in Texas history, he had built his own little town on the banks of the Pedernales south of Fredericksburg.

His two-story general store contained the post office, with Libbie Morris as postmaster, and a second-floor recreation room for dances and parties. Next door to the stone building, a drug store also served the community. Down the road, the schoolhouse with a steep, gabled roof and cupola became the center for church services, dramatic performances, musicals, and women's church societies. The town also had a hotel, roller mill, cotton gin, blacksmith shop, and homes for workers.

You can still see one of the large barns for the race horses, remains of the race track, and foundations of the hotel. The wide, white-frame front porches of the store are partially hidden by trees,

*New Yorker Francis Morris built his own little town on the banks of the Pedernales south of Fredericksburg in the late 1800s. Here he raised race horses and served the community with a handsome, two-story general store and recreation hall.*

*In Bertram, the A. B. McGill store faces the railroad track as it has since 1905. Bertram children bought their Buster Brown shoes here, and some knew the young midget whose real name was Johnny Clifton, a Bertram native.*

but it is still a beautiful setting with a rich history. The store now belongs to the T. E. Kennerly family, who use it as a residence.

## Nettie Whipple's General Merchandise Store, Roxton (Lamar County)

Nettie Whipple was ninety-three years old when she decided she couldn't run her general merchandise store in Roxton any more. For many years she had come every day to her big brick store building, facing the railroad tracks in the little country town of Roxton. She closed her doors for the last time in September of 1984.

Within a few months, dust began settling on the merchandise left inside. Little stools where women sat to watch Nettie measure out yards of fabric stood empty. An old sewing machine with a piece of cloth still under the needle looked as if the seamstress would be back in just a few minutes.

While Nettie ran the store, it was filled with Roxton shoppers looking for a good cut of meat, a jar of her own honey from the hives in her back yard, some bars of P&G soap, or a shade of just the right thread to match the bright-colored piece goods the ladies were buying.

No one wants to run Nettie's store today, and most of her former customers now shop in larger towns. As it is with many such stores all over the country, no one comes into Nettie Whipple's General Merchandise any more.

## Old Wells Store (Liberty County)

From the early 1800s, the Nacogdoches-Lynch-burg Trail was traveled by wagons and cattle through East Texas. Eight miles south of present-day Cleveland, a general store, blacksmith shop, cotton gin, grist mill, and wagon shop served travelers stopping at the grove of live oak trees.

Around 1875, D. D. Proctor & Company built a frame store in the community there known as Tarkington's Prairie. It became the settlement's post office, voting poll, credit house, and meeting place for many years. Other owners in the following years included the names of Lowe, Simmons, Pruitt, and Williams. It became the Wells Store in 1933.

Although it bears a Texas historical medallion, it has not operated as a store since about 1955. The present owners are Mr. and Mrs. Lawrence Going, who willingly share the store with visitors.

Inside, many of the original merchandise items and furnishings keep the feel of the days when people sat on the Masonic Lodge bench on the front porch and visited by the long, oak counter inside. Alongside the store, traces of the nineteenth-century wagon and cattle trail can still be seen.

*Although closed for business, Mr. and Mrs. Lawrence Going will happily show the Old Wells Store to travelers. It bears a historical medallion because of its location on the Nacogdoches-Lynchburg Trail.*

## Koocksville Store (Mason County)

The community of Koocksville, on the edge of Mason at the north edge of the Texas Hill Country, acquired its name after William Koock built a one-room log store in 1867. Koock and his wife Minna, both natives of Germany, lived in the store until they moved into their second store, a frame structure, and then into the two-story rock store built in the 1870s.

Koocksville was on the Texas-to-Kansas cattle trail during the cattle-driving era of the 1880s. Koock did an extensive trade with cattle and sheep ranchers and cattle buyers, selling groceries, ammunition, guns, furniture, drugs, and whiskey. On a good day, the store netted as much as $1,000. Besides purchasing supplies, customers could obtain credit and deposit their gold for safekeeping.

Upstairs, the community enjoyed regular dances as Koock made his store the center for townspeople to enjoy. He built a well outside and a playground for the children and was in the process of

*William Koock built this two-story rock store in the 1870s to trade with cattle and sheep ranchers and cattle buyers on their way to Kansas. It is located on the edge of Mason on the northern edge of the Hill Country.*

*The Old Rock Store has been a landmark for travelers en route to Austin ever since it was built in 1898. In the early days, Oak Hill was considered a separate town.*

building a rock house for his family when he was killed in a riding accident. After the store closed, Koocksville declined, but today its two-and-a-half-foot walls remain as a testimony of one pioneer storekeeper's faith in his town.

## Old Rock Store
## Oak Hill, Austin (Travis County)

Oak Hill is considered a part of Austin by most people, but when limestone was being shipped from the quarries here to the state capitol grounds in 1882, it was considered another town. The first settlements here were known as Live Oak Springs then Live Oak and Oatmanville. In 1900 it became Oak Hill.

The Old Rock Store has long been a landmark for travelers along this route. Influenced by the style of German rock buildings of Central Texas, the store was built in 1898 by James Andrew Patton, a former Texas Ranger, known affectionately as "The Mayor of Oak Hill." He also served as the community's postmaster and ran the store for a number of years. In the early days, Woodmen of the World had a lodge hall upstairs.

The store bears a Texas historical medallion.

# Bibliography

Bragonier, Reginald, and David Fisher. *What's What, A Visual Glossary of the Physical World.* Maplewood, NJ: Hammond, Inc., 1981.

Casey, Clifford. *Mirages, Mysteries, and Reality — Brewster County, Texas — The Big Bend of the Rio Grande.* Seagraves: Pioneer Book Publishing, Inc., 1972.

Cherokee County Historical Commission. *Cherokee County History.* Jacksonville: 1986.

"Crossroads to Progress — Grapeland — The Queen City of the Sand Flats." *The Grapeland Messenger,* 1972.

Day, James, ed. *The Texas Almanac 1857–1873.* Waco: The Texian Press, 1967.

Debo, Darrell. *Burnet — A Pioneer History, 1847–1881.* Vol. 1. Burnet: Eakin Publications, 1979.

Dooley, Betty, and Claude Dooley. *Why Stop? A Guide to Texas Historical Markers.* Houston: Gulf Publishing Company, 1985.

Engel, Alfred. *The Family of Andreas Engel.* Published by the author.

Fehrenbach, T. R. *Lone Star: A History of Texas and the Texans.* New York: American Legacy Press, 1983.

Fowler, William. "A Hundred Years to a Day." *TAMS Journal,* February 1983.

Frankston Bicentennial Commission. *Frankston and Its Neighbors: The Story Of Frankston, Texas and Neighboring Communities 1900–1976.* Jacksonville: Jayroe Graphic Arts, 1976.

Hale, Leon. "Catchin' Up on Some Country Store Sitting." *Houston Post,* Vol. 26, No. 8, December 11, 1985.

Hamrick, Alma Ward. *The Call of San Saba — A History of San Saba County.* San Felipe Press, 1969.

Hesterly, Wayne. *On the Street in Chappell Hill.* Published by the author, March 1984.

Howard, Dr. Rex A. *Texas Guidebook.* Amarillo: F. M. McCarty Company, 1970.

Hurt, Harry III. "The Store That Made Jonesville Famous." *Texas Monthly,* July 1982.

Kingston, Mike, ed. *Texas Almanac Sesquicentennial Edition.* Dallas: Dallas Morning News, 1985.

Kowert, Elise. "A Look Back — Fredericksburg 140/Texas 150 — Keepsake Edition." *Fredericksburg Standard-Radio Post,* June 11, 1986.

Lotto, F. *Fayette County — Her History and Her People.* Schulenburg: Sticker Steam Press, 1902.

McIlvain, Myra Hargrave. *Central Texas Auto Tours.* Austin: Eakin Publications, 1980.

———. *Texas Auto Trails, The South.* Austin: University of Texas Press, 1985.

———. *Texas Auto Trails, The Southeast.* Austin: University of Texas Press, 1982.

Madison, Virginia. *The Big Bend Country.* Albuquerque: University of New Mexico Press, 1955.

*Mason County News.* Sesquicentennial edition, 1986. G. S. Lyon, publisher.

Mayfield, Bernard. *Vanishing Towns of Cherokee County.* Published by the author, 1983.

Miller, Ray. *Eyes of Texas Travel Guide: Dallas/East Texas Edition.* Houston: Cordovan Corporation, 1978.

Moore, Bill. *Bastrop County.* Wichita Falls: Nortex Press, 1977.

Moore, Jack. *The History of Dialville.* Jacksonville: Published by the author, 1985.

Moursand, John Stribling. *Blanco County History.* Wichita Falls: Nortex, 1979.

Nelson, Sarah. "McGill Recalls Days Gone By." *The Highlander,* March 21, 1985.

Parker County Historical Commission. *History of Parker County.* Dallas: Taylor Publishing Company, 1980.

Parvin, Bob. "Country Store." *Texas Highways,* January 1976.

Porterfield, Bill. "It's All Over Now." *The Texas Observer,* July 10, 1970.

Rather, Dan. "The Last Grandmother." *The Fayette County Record,* March 4, 1986.

Rosston Historic Committee. *Rosston Centennial — 1872–1972.*

Ruff, Ann. *Traveling Texas Borders.* Houston: Gulf Publishing Company, 1983.

St. Clair, Clifton, and Kathleen St. Clair. *Little Towns of Texas.* Jacksonville: Jayroe Graphic Arts, 1982.

San Saba County Historical Commission. *San Saba County History, 1856–1983,* 1983.

Scott, Zelma. *A History of Coryell County, Texas.* Austin: Texas State Historical Association, 1965.

Shannon, Kelley. "Old-Fashioned Charm — Quiet Life Attracts Visitors to Maydelle." *Palestine Herald Press,* December 27, 1985.

Sharpe, Patricia, and Robert S. Waddell. *Texas Monthly Guidebook to Texas.* Austin: Texas Monthly Press, 1982.

Smithers, W. D. *Chronicles of the Big Bend.* Austin: Madrona Press, 1979.

*Southern Living,* Vol. 19, No. 11, November 1984.

Stambaugh, J. Lee. *History of Collin County.* Austin: Texas State Historical Commission, 1958.

Syers, Ed. *Backroads of Texas.* Houston: Gulf Publishing Company, 1985.

*Texas Almanac for 1857, a 1986 Facsimile Reproduction.* Dallas: Dallas Morning News, 1986.

*Texas Highways,* Vol. 26, No. 8, August 1979.

*That Fabulous Century — 60 Years of American Life 1900–1910.* New York: Time-Life Books, 1969.

Wayend, Leonie. "Early History of Fayette County, 1822–1865." Burnet: Eakin, 1979.

Webb, Walter Prescott, ed. *The Handbook of Texas.* 2 vols. Austin: Texas State Historical Association, 1952.

Whalen, Ken. "Neches Museum Houses Treasure Trove of Early Texas Memorabilia." *Tyler Courier-Telegraph,* May 18, 1986.

Zelade, Richard. *Texas Monthly Guide to the Hill Country.* Austin: Texas Monthly Press, 1983.

# Index

www.ingramcontent.com/pod-product-compliance
Lightning Source LLC
LaVergne TN
LVHW081321060426
835509LV00015B/1616